PUFFIN BOOKS

THE WILD WISDOM QUIZ BOOK: VOLUME 2

The World Wide Fund for Nature-India is one of the largest conservation organizations engaged in wildlife and nature conservation in our country. Wild Wisdom, an initiative of WWF-India, is the only nationwide wildlife quiz in the country, running into its 9th edition this year.

Also in Puffin by WWF-India

The Wild Wisdom Quiz Book

the wild wisdom QUIZ BOOK

VOLUME 2

Research and Compilation by Payal Narain

Illustrations by Vandana Singh

PUFFIN BOOKS

PUFFIN BOOKS

USA | Canada | UK | Ireland | Australia
New Zealand | India | South Africa | China

Puffin Books is part of the Penguin Random House group of companies
whose addresses can be found at global.penguinrandomhouse.com

Published by Penguin Books India Pvt. Ltd
7th Floor, Infinity Tower C, DLF Cyber City,
Gurgaon 122 002, Haryana, India

Penguin
Random House
India

First published in Puffin by Penguin Books India 2016

ISBN 9780143333883

Typeset in DINPro by Manipal Digital Systems, Manipal
Printed at Replika Press Pvt. Ltd, India

www.penguinbooksindia.com

CONTENTS

vi

ABOUT WWF-INDIA

The World Wide Fund for Nature (WWF) is one of the world's largest and most respected conservation organizations, with a mission to conserve natural biodiversity, promote sustainable living and build a future in which humans live in harmony with nature.

In India, WWF has been functional since 1969 and has a national presence through a network of sixty offices, distributed across twenty Indian states. WWF-India addresses issues on conservation of biological diversity, protection of habitats, management and restoration of freshwater bodies, climate change mitigation and environment education.

Environment Education (EE) Division

Environment Education (EE) is one of the oldest divisions of WWF-India, and has been an integral part of its conservation efforts since the last forty-seven years. The Division works with school students and teachers in more than twenty Indian states through programmes, such as the Wild Wisdom Quiz, Ek Prithvi, One Planet Academy and the WWF Volunteers programme. EE aims to promote admiration for nature and instil conscientiousness towards the environment in students and citizens alike. It recognizes the role of students as major stakeholders and guardians of the future, and helps develop in them critical-thinking skills, a positive attitude and an inclination towards a sustainable lifestyle.

THE WILD WISDOM QUIZ

WWF-India's Wild Wisdom Quiz was launched in 2008 to inculcate a sense of pride towards India's rich biodiversity and introduce environmental awareness among students. Since its launch, it has scaled new heights with every subsequent year to become India's only national-level wildlife quiz.

Wild Wisdom is a unique opportunity to encourage students to gain knowledge and delve deeper into our incredible natural legacy, as a crucial step towards cultivating conscious custodians of the environment. The quiz is both interactive and imaginative, and the syllabus is nature itself!

A FLASHBACK

2008

> The quiz is launched in Delhi during Wildlife Week
> Participation by 32 schools from the NCR
> Red FM conducts a radio-based quiz

2009

> Participation by 278 schools from 13 cities across India
> Anchored by quizmaster Cyrus Sahukar
> Miss India Universe 2009, Ekta Chowdhry, attends as the chief guest

2010

> 18 cities
> 5000+ students
> Anchored by leading wildlife filmmaker, Mike Pandey

2011

> 17 cities
> 15,641 students
> Anchored by social activist and renowned classical dancer, Mallika Sarabhai
> The quiz goes online

2012

> Endorsed by the CBSE
> A radio-based quiz, Rainbow Genius, is conducted by FM Rainbow

2013

> Participation by 550 schools
> Doordarshan, the Government of India's broadcast channel, airs the quiz

2014

> Penguin Books India and WWF-India bring out a compilation of the content
> Discovery Kids airs the nationals on primetime TV

2015

> ~ 35000 registrations
> Supported by MoES and Discovery Kids
> Anchored by actor Arjun Kapoor

HALL OF FAME

YEAR	SCHOOL	CITY	WINNERS
2009	Bombay Scottish School	Mumbai	Jayant Andrew David Poorvi Bellur
2010	Bhavan's Newsprint Vidyalaya	Kerala	K. J. Jayadev Jacob Kunnathoor
2011	Geetanjali Senior Secondary School	Hyderabad	L. Arnav A. V. Lakshmy
2012	Pon Vidyashram	Chennai	Effy Oommen John Manoj Krishna
2013	Vidya Mandir Senior Secondary School	Chennai	Sai Vignesh A. Rohit
2014	L'ecole Chempaka	Trivandrum	Pooja Bijoy Aaron Dev Jose
2015	Vidya Niketan Public School	Chennai	P. Shriman R. Avnish

ACKNOWLEDGEMENTS

We would like to express our gratitude to all the people who provided the necessary support in putting this book together.

First and foremost, we would like to thank Penguin Books India for publishing and taking on this initiative. Thanks to Sohini Mitra for seeing this through.

Next, we would like to acknowledge Payal Narain for compiling this vast repository of knowledge on biodiversity, and providing the readers with a joyful read.

Great thanks to Vandana Singh who, with her beautiful illustrations, made the book come alive.

We would also like to thank Chetna Kaith and the Wild Wisdom support team, including the entire Environment Education team—who generously provided their meaningful inputs along with the inspiration and encouragement that was much-needed in bringing the book to its timely completion.

Radhika Suri
Director, Environment Education
WWF-India

INTRODUCTION

The One Planet We Call Home

As with all other living organisms, the earth has nurtured and sustained humans ever since they first evolved. Fossilized remains of the human species, dating back to the Pleistocene Epoch, when they diverged from chimpanzees, were first discovered in Africa. Carl Linnaeus, who named numerous other animals, also gave our species its scientific name, *Homo sapien*, which is Latin for 'wise man'.

Like all other animals, our well-being from the cradle to the grave depends on the earth's resources—the air we breathe, the water we drink and the soil we till. However, unlike other animals, we have domesticated and harvested plants as well as animals to serve and feed us. Unfortunately, we often appreciate them only when they benefit us. We treat nature and her bounty as if they are inexhaustible, to be used and abused as we deem fit.

Today, with the increasing human population and accelerated development, our demands from the earth's resources are escalating at an unsustainable rate. Clean air, water and land are growing scarce, and many wonderful plants and animals are reaching the brink of extinction even before we can discover their existence.

Through all the wild and wonderful facts and figures that you will discover in this book, we seek to inspire and encourage each one of you to find ways—however small or big—to do your bit so that you can tread lightly on our planet. Can we pledge to live up to our species-name and really be the wise ones?

I, _____ _____, pledge that from this day forward,

🐾 I will reduce my electricity use by switching off lights when they're not needed, and use energy-efficient light bulbs instead.
🐾 I will save water by using a bucket to bathe and wash cars, instead of showers or hosepipes.
🐾 I will plant seeds and nurture trees.
🐾 I will eat locally sourced, seasonal and fresh food and not packaged produce.
🐾 I will not use plastic and other use-and-throw products.
🐾 I will reuse, upcycle and recycle—turning my old things into something new and useful.
🐾 I will donate or resell my old things.
🐾 I will not drink water that is bottled in plastic packaging.
🐾 I will walk, cycle, and use public transport or carpool with friends.
🐾 I will only buy organic and sustainable products.

Signed _____
Dated _____

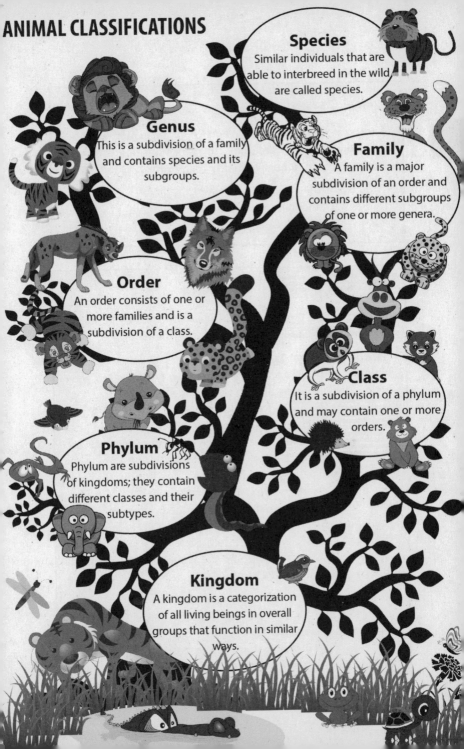

Animal Classifications

All living things are classified in a particular system, or biological rank, according to its similarities with and relationship to other animals. Today, the ranking scale followed is:

Domain → Kingdom → Phylum → Class → Order → Family → Genus → Species

A 24-Hour Geological Wristwatch

The Geological Wristwatch represents the history of life on earth, up to the present moment, as a single day.

Based on the radiometric dating of rocks, scientists estimate that the earth was formed 4.6 billion years ago, which marked the beginning of the Hadean Eon. Then a hot, molten mass, the earth gradually cooled over time. While the first unicellular life form probably appeared in the Archean Eon, multicellular life arrived in the Precambrian Era—with an explosion of new life forms in the Cambrian Period. Animal life started in the oceans and by the late Devonian Period, the first bony, four-limbed vertebrates adapted and subsequently dominated life on land. Dinosaurs ruled the earth in the Jurassic Period, but went extinct in the Cretaceous Period. So, contrary to popular Hollywood films, humans and dinosaurs never occupied the planet at the same time!

Modern humans evolved on earth only in the Holocene Epoch, about 11,000 years ago. In the 24-hour timescale, this period represents merely the final few seconds before midnight. But even this relatively short period has not prevented us from wreaking havoc on the natural world. Don't you think we need to stop the devastation and turn back the clock?

A 24 - HOUR GEOLOGICAL WRISTWATCH

Few seconds before midnight
Modern humans arrive; destruction follows

23:49 The great extinction event

23:40 Mass extinction of dinosaurs, but crocodilian and champsosaur reptiles survive

22:56 The first mammals appear

22:47 The first dinosaurs arrive

22:40 Mass extinction of insects

21:58 The first four-limbed vertebrates evolve

21:49 The first terrestrial plants grow

21:41 Appearance of the first bony fish

21:41 Molluscs and arthropods take over the seas

21:00 The Cambrian explosion; new life forms develop

Holocene Epoch
Pleistocene Epoch
Pliocene Epoch
Miocene Epoch
Oligocene Epoch
Eocene Epoch
Paleocene Epoch

CENOZOIC ERA
66 mya - present time
23:40 hrs -24:00 hrs

Cretaceous Period
Jurassic Period
Triassic Period

MEZOZOIC ERA
252 mya - 66 mya
22:40 hrs - 23:40 hrs

Clock face with hours 1–24 arranged around the dial.

01:01 The meteorite explosion

04:00 Unicellular life appears

05:30 Photosynthesis begins

13:00 The first eukaryotes appear

17:30 The first multicellular life appears

Permian Period
Carboniferous Period
Devonian Period
Silurian Period
Ordovician Period
Cambrian Period

PALEOZOIC ERA
542 mya - 252 mya
21: 10 hrs - 22:40 hrs

Proterozoic Eon
Archean Eon
Hadean Time

PRECAMBRIAN ERA
3.8 bya - 542 mya
04:10 hrs - 10:57 hrs

---

bya: a billion years ago*
mya: a million years ago*

*All timelines are estimates

SOIL

In the circle of life, from soil we arise and to soil we return; so important is this natural resource that even our home planet is named the earth. Imagine soil to be the skin of our planet—its upper layer a rich mixture that binds together complex elements to support life.

Evolved over millennia and of various types and textures, it performs many functions—it supports the growth and diversity of plant and animal life, stores and filters groundwater, is home to creatures great and small who help in decomposing matter, and creates habitats for new life forms. And that's not all! Sacred in various cultures, soil also contributes numerous gases to the earth's atmosphere, and provides livelihood to many—from artisans and architects to scientists and politicians.

However, as with all of earth's resources, soil is threatened by man-made pressures which results in loss of soil productivity and reduced food supply for people and wildlife.

Questions

1 Soil is a non-renewable resource and is formed over millennia. Which of these is the parent material of different types of soil?

   a. Quartz   **b.** Calcite

   c. Mica   **d.** All of these

2 Being irreversible, which of these is the most serious form of soil degradation?

   a. Nutrient Depletion   **b.** Acidification

   c. Erosion   **d.** Overgrazing

According to WWF, about half the earth's topsoil, rich in organic matter and nutrients, has been degraded in the last 150 years. This is mainly due to deforestation, overgrazing by domestic animals and the use of harmful agricultural practices.

3 High levels of acidity can stunt plant growth and reduce nutrient absorption. Which of the following is added to soil to reduce its acidity level?

   a. Ammonia

   b. Agricultural Lime

   c. Sulphur

   d. Iron

4 Which soil-forming process is most closely linked to the activities of living organisms?

   a. Hydration   **b.** Carbonation

   c. Eluviation   **d.** Decomposition

5 An important part of soil life, mycorrhiza is a mutually beneficial association between which of these?

   a. Animals and Fungi   **b.** Algae and Bacteria

   c. Plant and Fungi   **d.** Plant and Animal

Have you heard of a place called the Garden of the Gods? It is a designated National Natural Landmark (NNL) i.e., a site that preserves natural history in the United States of America. It has several unique red rock formations, including gigantic balancing rocks that illustrate the geological and ecological history of the region.

6 Which of these is the main ingredient of soil?

   a. Organic Matter

   b. Water

   c. Minerals

   d. All of these

7 Which of these soil types offers the best percolation?

   a. Sand

   b. Clay

   c. Silt

   d. Loam

Do you have shiny, strong teeth? You should know that your body needs phosphorus and calcium for healthy teeth and bones! Phosphorus is a mineral also found in phosphate deposits in sedimentary and igneous rocks. Do make sure to include phosphorus-rich plants like corn, oats, kidney beans and soya beans in your diet.

8 Tetanus, also called lockjaw, is characterized by muscular spasms and is caused by soil bacteria that enter the system through a cut or wound.
Which bacteria is this?

a. *Bacillus anthracis*

b. *Escherichia coli*

c. *Clostridium botulinum*

d. *Clostridium tetani*

9 Which unicellular animals living in soil have the ability to produce antibiotics like Streptomycin and Terramycin?

a. Fungi

b. Algae

c. Actinomycetes

d. Protozoa

10 Out of these great global spheres, which one represents soil?

a. Biosphere

b. Hydrosphere

c. Lithosphere

d. Pedosphere

11 A terrestrial or land ecosystem is made up of soil, primary producers and decomposers. Which of these are primary producers?

a. Grasses   **b.** Micro-organisms

c. Herbivores   **d.** Carnivores

12 Through various soil-forming processes, soil gets formed in several layers. What are these layers known as?

a. Horizons   **b.** Structures

c. Aggregates   **d.** Parent Material

13 Humus is vital for healthy soil. Which of these is an important nutrient contained in humus?

a. Mercury   **b.** Nitrogen

c. Lead   **d.** Iron

14 In which of these materials have well-preserved fossilized remains of plants and animals from the Triassic Period been found? Some of this excavated material even contains fragments of DNA.

a. Amber

b. Coal

c. Granite

d. Lava

Did you know that fossil evidence found deep in the soil indicate that the continents were once joined as one land mass, but later broke up into various parts? For example, fossils, of the reptile *Mesosaurus*, were found in South America as well as in Africa; additionally, there remains a similarity in the shape of the east coastline of South America and the west coast of Africa. These observations show that both these land masses were once joined together, but then broke up and drifted apart. This is known as the theory of continental drift.

15 Many animals eat soil as a method of self-medication. What is this practice called?
   a. Geophagia   **b.** Dysphagia
   c. Hyperphagia   **d.** Xerophagia

16 Of what is the earth's innermost core made?
   a. Nickel   **b.** Magnesium
   c. Iron   **d.** Fire

17 What is the colour of the soil—locally known as regur—which is clayey, rich in iron, but poor in nitrogen and organic matter?
   a. Red   **b.** Yellow
   c. Brown   **d.** Black

18 An animal that is specifically adapted to digging and living underground is _____.

a. Cursorial
b. Arboreal
c. Fossorial
d. Terrestrial

19 Under which category of soil fauna would the tiny springtail—0.2–2.0 mm in size—fall?

a. Microfauna
b. Mesofauna
c. Macrofauna
d. Megafauna

Did you know that, in 2014, a new species of springtail was found in Ladakh during the Cold Desert Expedition by the Zoological Survey of India (ZSI)? This was a joint discovery by scientists from the University of Navarra, Spain and those from ZSI.

20 Usually formed in warm, humid climates, which type of humus is likely to have the most earthworms?

a. Mor
b. Mull
c. Moder
d. All of these

21 A detritivore adds to soil richness by feeding on dead
plants or animals and their waste. Which of these
animals is a detritivore?

a. Snail
b. Mouse
c. Bat
d. Lizard

22 Most laterite soil is rusty-red and formed in
tropical areas. What lends this colour to laterite
soil?

a. Sulphur
b. Iron Oxides
c. Mica
d. Carbon Dioxide

23 In which branch of soil studies can we learn about
the formation, the types, the chemistry and the
structure of soil?

a. Pedology
b. Agronomy
c. Paleontology
d. Petrology

**New soil is created every day, but ever so slowly.
Experts estimate that in 500 to 1000 years, only
about an inch of new soil may be formed! So don't
treat soil like dirt—it's very precious.**

24 Which soil layer, usually rich in humus and other minerals, is of great value to life on earth?

  a. Topsoil

  b. Laterite Soil

  c. Subsoil

  d. Bedrock

25 Marble, quartzite, slate and schist are formed by extreme heat and pressure. To which type of rock do these belong?

  a. Igneous   **b.** Sedimentary

  c. Metamorphic   **d.** Meteorite

26 Important factors that affect soil formation are the shape and features of the landscape, also known as the _____.

  a. Zoography   **b.** Topography

  c. Geography   **d.** Cartography

27 Many species of animals, such as birds, bats, monkeys and deer, practise geophagy—the practice of eating earth for digestive benefits. Which type of soil do geophaghic animals prefer?

  a. Sand   **b.** Gravel

  c. Clay   **d.** Silt

Today, we have over seven billion people on our planet—all using the same resources. In India,

the population density per square km is
370 people—this is about ten times the world
average! You can see that this is a huge demand
from the land and its uses. But some people have
too much and some have too little. How many people
do you think the food, water and soil of India can
comfortably support?

28 Often made of limestone, what is the rock formation
that hangs from the ceiling of caves?
   a. Stalactite   b. Stalagmite
   c. Stack   d. Tor

29 In an experiment to show the suction capacity
of water in soil, two water-filled tubes of equal
diameter are also loaded with fine and coarse sand
each. Which soil type would show a
greater rise in the water level?
   a. Coarse Sand
   b. Fine Sand
   c. Both raise the water to the same level
   d. Neither raises the water level

30 Bones of the largest dinosaur that ever lived, the
Brachiosaurus, were first dug out of rocks near the
River _____.
   a. Narmada   b. Colorado
   c. Amazon   d. Yangtze

The Virunga Mountains are a chain of volcanic mountains in East Africa. Most of the volcanoes here are inactive, dormant or extinct—but some are still active. One of the volcanoes even has a lava lake in its crater. The Virunga National Park is a UNESCO World Heritage Site, and the home of the Critically Endangered (CR) Mountain Gorilla.

31 Which type of soil is made by insects, worms, fungi and bacteria?

a. Humus

b. Sandy

c. Volcanic

d. Clay

32 At around 60 per cent, which group of minerals is the most abundant in the earth's crust?

a. Quartz   **b.** Feldspars

c. Olivine   **d.** Mica

33 Used in gardens, what kind of soil is usually dark-coloured and very porous?

a. Rich Organic Soil   **b.** Poor Sandy Soil

c. Polluted Soil   **d.** Leached Soil

34 Which colour does humus impart to soil?

a. Yellow   **b.** Red

c. Brown   **d.** Black

The Grand Canyon, about 450 km long and 30 km wide in some parts, is one of the world's deepest gorges that has been carved out of layers of rock over millions of years by the fast-flowing River Colorado. Today, it stands like a geological clock that exposes a part of the earth's natural history set in the layers of stone.

35 What do earthworms do to improve the quality of the soil that they inhabit?

a. Decompose plant and animal matter

c. Improve water-holding capacity

b. Create channels for root growth

d. All of these

36 What is the basic unit of soil?

a. Lumen

b. Kelvin

c. Mole

d. Pedon

37 Himba tribal women from Namibia are famous for applying a paste of ochre and animal fat on their bodies for decoration purposes. What is the ore that is compounded in ochre, a naturally formed earth pigment?

a. Iron

b. Lead

c. Manganese

d. Gold

If you study to be a petrologist when you grow up, you will become an expert on all kinds of rocks! You'll

learn how they are formed, of what they are made
and even where each type of rock is found. Isn't that
an interesting career?

38 Which component of soil provides important
nutrients for plant growth?
- **a.** Clay
- **b.** Humus
- **c.** Rock
- **d.** Sand

39 The ancient Egyptians were prosperous because they
grew and traded crops like wheat, flax and papyrus.
These were grown in soil that was deposited after the
annual flooding of the River Nile. What type of soil
was this?
- **a.** Humus
- **b.** Silt
- **c.** Clay
- **d.** Sand

40 There lies a layer of hot, molten rock beneath the
earth's crust. What is this geothermal resource
called?
- **a.** Shale
- **b.** Magma
- **c.** Basalt
- **d.** Amber

Have you seen a picture of Uluru, also known as
Ayers Rock? Sacred to the Pitjantjatjara aboriginals,
it's one massive piece of red sandstone—about 350
m high, 3.6 km long and 1.9 km wide. This monolith,
once part of an ancient seabed, is now about
300 million years old!

41 Recently discovered in 2015, which fossilized species is thought to be an ancestor of humans?

    a. *Homo naledi*

    b. *Homo habilis*

    c. *Ramapithecus*

    d. *Sivapithecus*

In nature, rocks and minerals—molten at very high temperatures—exist beneath the earth's surface and may flow out of a crater as hot lava during a volcanic eruption.

42 What is the layer of the earth that comprises the ocean basins and the continents?

    a. Mantle   **b.** Liquid Outer Core

    c. Crust   **d.** Solid Inner Core

43 Which type of soil has the smallest grains—less than 0.002 mm in diameter—and can be observed only under a high-powered microscope?

    a. Silt   **b.** Clay

    c. Sand   **d.** Gravel

44 Which symbol is used to denote the layer of bedrock in soil?

    a. A   **b.** B

    c. C   **d.** R

45 When is World Soil Day celebrated each year?
   a. 5 March
   b. 5 June
   c. 5 September
   d. 5 December

The United Nations dedicated 2015 as the 'Year of Soil' to raise awareness about soil and its importance in our lives. On this occasion, José Graziano da Silva, the director general of the Food and Agricultural Organization of the UN, said, 'The multiple roles of soils often go unnoticed. Soils don't have a voice, and few people speak out for them. They are our silent ally in food production.'

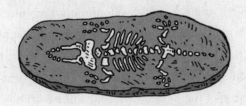

Answers

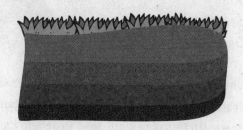

1. **d. All of these**
    Rocks and sedimentary material found on and below the earth's surface are processed by weather and other factors for soil formation. Over a long period of time, due to cycles of extreme heat and cold, large rocks split, and chemical and organic developments take place to form layers of matter in the earth's crust. Different types of material, including minerals, water, air, plant and animal particles, combine to form soil. The parent material determines the kind of soil that will eventually form and its fertility.

2. **c. Erosion**
    Wrong use or overuse leads to the ruin or loss of soil. Some of the threats to soil are erosion, desertification and salinization. Of these, soil erosion is considered the most harmful because when erosion happens on a large scale, its effects cannot be reversed. Natural soil erosion,

due to the action of wind and water, does take place over time. However, increased human activities are causing soil erosion on a massive scale and at an accelerated rate. Cutting down trees and clearing forests that shelter as well as bind the earth causes soil to be left exposed to rain and wind. This results in rapid erosion. With less soil to absorb rainwater, there is excessive run-off into rivers—which can cause flooding and, consequently, even more erosion.

3. b. **Agricultural Lime**

4. d. **Decomposition**

5. c. **Plant and Fungi**
    There is a symbiotic mycorrhizal relationship between fungi and the roots of the host plant. The fungus gains access to carbohydrates, while providing phosphorus and stored nitrogen to the plant when needed. This association forms a key component of soil chemistry.

6. d. **All of these**

7. a. **Sand**

8. d. *Clostridium tetani*

9. c. **Actinomycetes**
    These are a type of bacteria that are branch-shaped and live in soil. Some of these can cause diseases, while others are the source of antibiotics.

10. **d. Pedosphere**

11. **a. Grasses**

12. **a. Horizons**

13. **b. Nitrogen**

14. **a. Amber**

Amber is a thick liquid resin which oozed out of ancient trees and hardened into a rock-like substance that did not decay. Rare and beautiful, it's an expensive gemstone, and is found in various colours—although, usually, it's honey-gold or amber in colour. Paleontologists value it because it tells the story of the earth's history—of insects and other living creatures that existed millions of years ago, trapped in the sticky liquid before it solidified into a translucent lump. Well-preserved remains of plants and animals in amber, from the Triassic Period, have been found.

15. **a. Geophagia**

16. **c. Iron**

17. **d. Black**

18. **c. Fossorial**

Animals that have evolved to live mainly below the surface of the ground are called fossorial animals. These include a wide variety of species, such as worms and hornets, snakes and frogs, marmots and moles. While some of these may live, breed and feed underground, others may be partly fossorial i.e., they may live and give birth underground, but come above ground to feed and breed.

19. b. Mesofauna

20. b. Mull
Mull humus is mainly found in warm and wet deciduous forests as well as grasslands. It consists of well-mixed soil that is porous and crumbly, and is rich in organic and mineral matter. This soil is alkaline and abundant in organisms like bacteria and earthworms.

21. a. Snail

22. b. Iron Oxides

23. a. Pedology

24. a. Topsoil

25. c. Metamorphic
Metamorphic rocks are formed when pre-existing rocks, being exposed to extreme heat and pressure, undergo chemical and physical changes.

26. b. Topography

27. c. Clay

28. a. Stalactite
Stalactites are interesting mineral formations that hang like pointed swords from the ceiling of caves. They are usually created by the constant drip of water drops

mixed with minerals. Stalagmites, on the other hand, are icicle-shaped formations that rise from the floor of the caves, produced by the precipitation of water and minerals dripping from the ceiling. In India, one can spot spectacular stalactites and stalagmites in Belum Caves, Andhra Pradesh.

29. a. **Coarse Sand**

30. b. **Colorado**
The deep canyon carved by the Colorado River, over millions of years, tells the fantastic story of the earth's natural history, layer by layer. Hiking down its steep sides from the Colorado Plateau to the riverside, one can travel through time—from the Chinle Formation of the Triassic Period up to the granite Vishnu Basement Rocks of the Proterozoic Period. Thousands of marine and terrestrial fossils, including parts of the *Brachiosaurus's* skeleton, have been found embedded in the rocks of the Grand Canyon.

31. a. **Humus**

32. b. **Feldspars**

33. a. **Rich Organic Soil**

34. d. **Black**

35. d. **All of these**
Earthworms are annelids that have been called 'ecosystem engineers' since they are responsible for

restructuring the habitat in which they live. They create channels for air, water and plant-roots underground; they also succeed in mixing layers of the soil despite their tiny size. Because of this, Charles Darwin called earthworms 'nature's ploughs'. Furthermore, they decompose organic material and enrich the soil with their waste matter. The Earthworm Society of Britain works for the conservation of and awareness about these important animals.

36. d. Pedon

37. a. Iron

Ochre is one of the most commonly found earth pigments, and contains iron oxide. It is found in shades of yellow, red, purple, brown and dark brown. The 'otjize' paste, composed of red ochre mined from Kaokoland, protects their skin from the exceedingly hot and dry climate of Namibia. The mixture is usually aromatic as it is perfumed using a local shrub, and tinges the skin and hair with a deep red-orange colour. This lends the clan a distinctive appearance.

38. b. Humus

39. b. Silt

40. b. Magma

41. a. _Homo naledi_

In 2013, two amateur cave explorers discovered a treasure trove of fossil bones on the floor of a cave, buried in the clayey soil of a deep chamber, near Johannesburg, South Africa. The bones were excavated from the Dinaledi Chamber of the Rising Star cave system—part of the World Heritage Site, the Cradle of Humankind. This chamber could only be accessed by very slim people— mainly women—through a narrow passage nicknamed the Superman's Crawl. The bones were later identified as the remains of an ancient relative of humans and chimpanzees. About 1550 bones and bone fragments were found, then pieced together to form the skeleton of this ancestor. Although there are differing opinions, this new but extinct species was described in 2015.

42. c. Crust

43. b. Clay

44. d. R

45. d. 5 December

PLANTS

Plants, of the kingdom Plantae, include some of the largest as well as the tiniest organisms.

Fossil evidence suggests that early plants evolved in water billions of years ago, possibly in the Pre-Cambrian Age; this was followed by plants that grew on land, including flowering plants and grasses. It was only after the spread of grasslands that true carnivores and herbivores appeared on the planet.

Plants provide shelter, food and medicine to animals, including humans. They regulate the water cycle, produce oxygen and absorb carbon dioxide. They also bind and enrich the soil. Plants offer us recreational pleasure; they are of religious significance and cultural value as well, having been a source of inspiration for works of art and literature for centuries!

Early humans lived in harmony with this precious part of nature and we need to do the same if we hope to continue enjoying its many benefits.

Questions

1 Which is the national organization responsible for the regular monitoring and assessment of the forest resources of India?
   a. Forest Survey of India
   b. Forest Research Institute
   c. Wildlife Institute of India
   d. Indira Gandhi National Forest Academy

2 Solar energy is stored in the form of food in leaves with the help of _____.
   a. Chlorophyll   **b.** Ammonia
   c. Carbon   **d.** Nitrogen

According to records of Indian, Chinese, Egyptian, Roman and Greek civilizations, wildlife, especially plants, have been used for medicinal purposes since ancient times. In India's Terai belt, an old saying goes, 'No jungles, no healing'.

3 Which of these 'specified plants', protected under the Wildlife (Protection) Act, 1972, is one not allowed to grow without a license?
   a. Blue Vanda   **b.** Red Vanda
   c. Lady's Slipper Orchid   **d.** All of these

4 Truffle, highly prized by gourmets, is the fruiting body of a type of fungus that grows _____.

a. On trees
b. In water
c. Underground
d. All of these

5 Which of the following is the tallest and thickest grass?

a. Congress Grass
b. Moonjh
c. Bamboo
d. Sugarcane

6 Which herbicide was aerially sprayed as a biological warfare tactic by the US, in order to destroy jungles and crops that provided cover to the Viet Cong? This action had a hugely negative impact on forests, crops, biodiversity and human health.

a. Agent Orange
b. DDT
c. Variola
d. Agent Matrix

Most of you know about the fictitious Mandrake in the Harry Potter series—it was a strange plant that the Hogwarts students studied in their herbology class. The scream of a fully grown plant could kill! Have

you studied the real Mandrake in your botany class?
The plant has poisonous roots and leaves.

7 Chlorophyll is critical for photosynthesis, a process that produces usable chemical energy in plants. What is the loss of chlorophyll—leading to the yellowing of leaves—called?
   a. Chlorosis
   b. Chlorophilia
   c. Chlorination
   d. Osmosis

8 An invasive species is one that is non-native to the habitat and causes harm to the environment in which it is introduced. Which of these plants is not an invasive species?
   a. *Lantana camara*
   b. *Prosopis juliflora*
   c. *Parthenium hysterophorus*
   d. *Prosopis cineraria*

9 The Kurinjimala Sanctuary was set up in 2006 for the protection of the Neelakurinji, a shrub bearing vivid purplish-blue flowers. Where is it located in India?
   a. Tamil Nadu   **b.** Maharashtra
   c. Kerala   **d.** Karnataka

10 Certain plants are adapted to a particular environment; which kind of plants characterizes a riparian or riverbank zone?
   a. Hydrophilic plants
   b. Xerophytic plants
   c. Epiphytic plants
   d. Halophytic plants

11 Which of these is a carnivorous plant?
   a. Sundew
   b. Lady's Slipper Orchid
   c. Neelakurinji
   d. Rhododendron

> The fruit of the Fishberry plant, a climbing vine found in India, is toxic to fish. The powder made from the dried fruit was used for fishing; when put into water, it stuns the fish, which can then be easily caught.

12 Used in Ayurveda, Unani and in Siddha medicine, which of these plants has a strong case for possessing anti-cancer properties?
   a. Tulsi
   b. Banyan
   c. Betel Leaf
   d. Areka Nut

13 A living museum mainly restricted to small parts of Kerala, which of these is one of the most endangered primeval forest ecosystems in India?
   a. Sholas
   b. Terai
   c. Myristica Swamps
   d. Mangrove

14 Which is the larval host plant of the silk-producing moth, *Bombyx mori*?

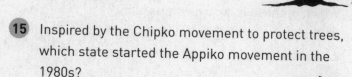

a. Mulberry

b. Neem

c. Rhododendron

d. All of these

15 Inspired by the Chipko movement to protect trees, which state started the Appiko movement in the 1980s?

a. Uttarakhand

b. Madhya Pradesh

c. Andhra Pradesh

d. Karnataka

16 Which tree, also the state tree of Manipur, famous for its red-brown wood, is popular for making musical instruments?

a. Banyan   b. Neem

c. Deodar   d. Indian Mahogany

In January 2016, the Zinnia—an edible flower—was the first flower to bloom in the vegetable laboratory on board the NASA International Space Station.

17 The Shola ecosystem consists of _____.

a. Mangroves interspersed with deciduous trees

b. Grasslands interspersed with thorny scrub

c. Montane grasslands interspersed with evergreen forests

d. Mudflats interspersed with grass

18 What is the symbiotic relationship between the fig wasp and the fig tree known as?

a. Mutualism

b. Commensalism

c. Parasitism

d. Competition

19 Which of these trees can grow on another tree for support, and may even eventually strangle and kill the supporting tree?

a. Peepul

b. Banyan

c. Pilkhan

d. All of these

Trees have held an important position since time immemorial. Tablets from the Indus Valley civilization, roughly dating back to 2500 BC, show trees growing on a pedestal and fenced in, as is often noticed in villages and temples.

20 What are lichens commercially used for?

a. Detergent

b. Glue

c. Dye

d. Fuel

21 Which material, a major cause of forest fires, is now being used in biomass gasifiers to generate electricity in Berinag, a village in Uttarakhand?

a. Deer Dung
b. Pine Needles
c. Shed Feathers
d. Driftwood

22 Just thirty years ago, rainforests of the world's third and sixth largest islands were teeming with elephants, rhinos, tigers, apes and birds. However, this has largely been destroyed by global agricultural, paper and pulp industries. Which islands are these?

a. Madagascar and Mauritius
b. Sumatra and Borneo
c. Java and Sumatra
d. Papua New Guinea and Solomon Islands

23 In India, herbivores avoid its leaves but butterflies and birds are regular visitors for its flowers and berries. This plant, an aggressive colonizer, is listed as one of the worst weeds in the world. It is the _____.

a. Balsam
b. Ipomoea
c. Bougainvillea
d. Lantana

While plant-watching in the Western Ghats, you
might spot a shrub with deep-green leaves and an
occasional large white one that is a specialized leaf!
This plant is called the Dhobi's Kerchief. It also has
small orange flowers that are seasonal.

24 Which of these innovative products was invented by
the Swiss engineer, George de Mestral, after studying
how burs worked?
  a. Post-its
  b. Velcro
  c. Double-sided tape
  d. All of these

25 Bael, the state tree of Puducherry, is commonly
eaten for stomach disorders. What is another name
for this tree?
  a. Breadfruit Tree
  b. Wood Apple Tree
  c. Ironwood Tree
  d. Jackfruit Tree

26 In plant cultivation, what is known as hydroponics?
  a. Growing plants without water
  b. Growing plants by playing music for them
  c. Growing plants with soil and water
  d. Growing plants in a nutrient solution without soil

Did you know that the Mustard Tree, or Peelu,
which is found in dry and arid regions of the Indian
subcontinent, is also called the Toothbrush Tree?

People chew on the twigs as this is supposed to improve dental hygiene by preventing gum disease and tooth decay.

27 Which of these well-known trees, often incorrectly called the Flame of the Forest, is not a native Indian species?

a. Silk Cotton Tree   **b.** Palash

c. Gulmohar   **d.** Laburnum

28 Which of the following plants is used for making liquid biofuel?

a. Palm Oil   **b.** Sugarcane

c. Wheat   **d.** Jatropha

29 Which of these crops is responsible for large-scale deforestation and destruction of the rainforest habitat in Indonesia and Malaysia, and for putting species like the orangutan at severe risk of extinction?

a. Coconut   **b.** Eucalyptus

c. Banana   **d.** Oil Palm

30 The Himalayan Cedar is an evergreen pine tree, native to the Western Himalayan region. What is it also known as?

a. Kail   **b.** Bakul

c. Chir Pine   **d.** Deodar

31 What type of plant is the thorny Khejri tree, which is well-adapted to the desert conditions of Rajasthan?

a. Epiphyte

b. Lithophyte

c. Halophyte

d. Xerophyte

The *Drosera* is a perennial plant that you can spot in parts of the Konkan region. It uses a sticky liquid on its tentacles to trap insects.

32 Ounce for ounce, the fruit and leaves of this miracle tree are said to have three times the iron found in spinach, calcium that is equal to four glasses of milk, vitamin C that is equal to seven oranges, and potassium that is equal to three bananas. Which Indian tree is this?

a. Drumstick Tree

b. Gulmohar Tree

c. Laburnum Tree

d. Tamarind Tree

The Fishtail Palm is so called because its triangular leaflets, which face each other on either side of the stem, look like the tail fin of a fish. The fruit hang in tassel-like bunches and look like a huge ponytail. Have you seen a palm tree like this?

33 Plants obtain most of their nutrients from the soil. Which of these is not an important plant food?

a. Nitrogen

b. Keratin

c. Phosphorus

d. Potassium

34 Which of these is a plant that is not from India? An invasive species, it spreads quickly and causes local plants and animals to die.

a. Water Lily   b. Water Hyacinth

c. Lotus   d. Elephant Grass

35 Native to India, used in cooking and in medicine, what is the fragrant Malabar Grass also known as?

a. Lemongrass

b. Cymbopogon

c. Citronella Grass

d. All of these

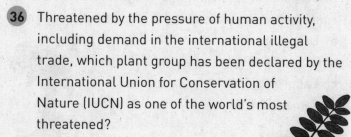

36 Threatened by the pressure of human activity, including demand in the international illegal trade, which plant group has been declared by the International Union for Conservation of Nature (IUCN) as one of the world's most threatened?

a. Conifers

b. Cacti

c. Ficus

d. Mosses

37 Which of these trees is deciduous i.e., it sheds its leaves seasonally?

a. Mango   b. Teak

c. Neem   d. Jackfruit

The Whomping Willow was a magical violent tree that featured in the Harry Potter series. Did you notice that it was deciduous?

38 The name of which Indian state stands for 'the land of forests'?

a. Uttarakhand   **b.** Meghalaya

c. Jharkhand   **d.** Himachal Pradesh

39 Though we use it as a vegetable in cooking, mushrooms are a type of _____.

a. Plant

b. Fungi

c. Algae

d. Moss

40 Under which species of tree did Mahavira, the 24th Tirthankara of the Jains, attain enlightenment?

a. Peepul   **b.** Sal

c. Banyan   **d.** Teak

41 This disease causes discolouration and death in plant tissue, including that of the tomato and potato. Which disease is this?

a. Crown Gall

b. Scabies

c. Boll Rot

d. Blight

42 Which of these is the largest living species of a tree with a single trunk?

a. Banyan   b. Grand Fir

c. Giant Sequoia   d. Sitka Spruce

43 Native to India, the *Alstonia scholaris* is also called the Indian Blackboard Tree. Wood from this tree was mainly used to make wooden slates. What is another common name for the Indian Blackboard?

a. Indian Silk Cotton Tree   b. Flame of the Forest

c. Indian Devil Tree   d. Indian Rosewood Tree

The Baobab is an odd-looking tree—it has a very thick trunk but thin, straggly, root-like branches bunched at the top. There are only nine species of the Baobab found in the world, out of which six are found only in Madagascar.

44 Which plant flowers in large numbers after a long period of time—about once every forty-eight years—and causes an increase in the rat population because the rodents feed on its fruit?

a. Banana

b. Cotton

c. Bamboo

d. Pumpkin

45 Now widely cultivated, *Jatropha curcas*, or the Physic Nut, is a flowering shrub that is used to produce biodiesel. To which country is it native?

a. India
b. Mexico
c. China
d. Australia

46 It is usually difficult to grow vegetables in highly alkaline soil but which of these plants grows well in it?

a. Potato
b. Peanut
c. Radish
d. Asparagus

47 Lichen is an organism that results from the mutually beneficial relationship between which two organisms?

a. Metazoa and Fungi
b. Protozoa and Soil
c. Cyanobacteria and Fungi
d. Plants and Animals

48 Essential to the ancient Aztecs, which plant species was domesticated by humans over 9000 years ago from its wild ancestor, a Mexican grass called Teosinte? It is highly valued in the modern world.

a. Rice
b. Potato
c. Maize
d. Cotton

Fibre from the valuable jute plant is spun and woven into cloth. In some countries, the leaves too are utilized—to make soup.

49 Which organism can grow in areas too harsh for most others, such as bare rock, desert sand, dead wood, animal bones and rusty metal?

a. Orchids **b.** Lichens

c. Moss **d.** Mushrooms

50 As per the India State of Forest Report 2015, by the Forest Survey of India (FSI), which state has the largest forest cover area—of about 77, 462 sq. km?

a. Uttarakhand **b.** Madhya Pradesh

c. Kerala **d.** Mizoram

51 The layer of soil where most plants grow is called _____.

a. Topsoil **b.** Gravel

c. Subsoil **d.** Bedrock

52 Match the state with its state flower:

Lotus	Arunachal Pradesh
Palash	Bihar
Pot Marigold	Andhra Pradesh
Lady's Slipper Orchid	Karnataka
Water Lily	Madhya Pradesh

53 A food source for butterflies, and also used for medicinal purposes, this beautiful Himalayan plant is the state flower of Himachal Pradesh and the national flower of Nepal. Which flower is this?

> **In 2015, a new species of wild banana,
> *Musa indandamanensis*, with orange-coloured pulp,
> was found growing in a remote tropical forest of
> the Andaman and Nicobar Islands. This species was
> discovered by a scientist of the Botanical Survey
> of India (BSI).**

54 This tree was brought to India by the Portuguese, and now grows in Goa, Maharashtra, and parts of south India. The seed is a tasty snack and is also used in cooking. Which tree is this?

55 Which country has the greatest percentage of its land area under forest cover?

Answers

1. a. **Forest Survey of India**

2. a. **Chlorophyll**

3. d. **All of these**

   All these plant species are protected under Schedule VI of the Wildlife (Protection) Act. No one is allowed to buy, sell or cultivate these plants without prior permission. Although there are only six wild Indian plants which have been named under Schedule VI, there are many more that are threatened.

4. c. **Underground**

   A truffle is a wild fungus. Some species are greatly prized in several international cuisines. Aromatic and extremely expensive, truffles are used in small quantities. The fungi are found in close proximity to the roots of trees. Truffle-hunting is an activity in which trained 'truffle hogs' and 'truffle dogs'

sniff out the fungi. In December 2014, about 1.89 kg sold for around US $61,000.

5.   c. Bamboo

6.   a. Agent Orange
Made by Monsanto Corporation and the Dow Chemical Company, Agent Orange was sprayed from the air by the US army during the Vietnam War. It was so named because the herbicide was stored in drums that were painted with orange and white stripes. It was a highly toxic defoliant that destroyed all crops, bushes and forests where it was sprayed. This was done so that the Viet Cong soldiers would have no place to hide, and could easily be spotted and shot by American soldiers. Thousands of soldiers died due to exposure to this toxin and thousands of civilians continued to suffer for decades afterwards from severe health problems, including cancer, Hodgkin's disease and skin diseases. Millions of acres of tropical forests were destroyed beyond repair, and animals like elephants, tigers, leopards, gibbons, cranes and many others lost their habitat and their lives.

7.   a. Chlorosis

8.   d. *Prosopis cineraria*
A plant or animal introduced to a new environment which it affects adversely is called an invasive species. In

India, *Lantana camara*, *Prosopis juliflora* and *Parthenium hysterophorus* have all been introduced from foreign countries and have harmed the native plant and animal diversity. *Prosopis cineraria*, also called Khejri, is a native Indian tree that has adapted to hot, dry habitats, including deserts. It is an important source of fodder and the pods are cooked like a vegetable. It is similar in appearance to *Prosopis juliflora* and is sometimes confused with this invasive plant.

9. c. Kerala

10. a. Hydrophilic plants

Hydrophytes, or hydrophilic plants, grow in water and in riparian zones—which include riverbanks and other wetland areas. Native Indian trees, like the mango, jamun and arjun, prefer areas with perennial streams and water sources when they are found growing in the wild.

11. a. Sundew

Flowers like the sundew belong to the genus of plants called *Drosera*. There are numerous species of *Drosera*, some of which are found in India. Carnivorous herbs, they trap insects with sticky hair-like structures that grow on their leaves. Once the fly is stuck, the leaves curl up around the prey so that it cannot escape and the plant can consume it slowly. In India, this plant is also used to produce traditional medicine.

12. a. Tulsi

13. c. Myristica Swamps
The Myristica Swamp ecosystem consists of marshy, evergreen forests. Today, the remains are highly fragmented and disappearing fast. Much of the area has been cleared for cultivating rice and some parts are submerged under lakes created by dams. Small patches are still found in Karnataka and Kerala. The swamps are abundant in trees, shrubs, herbs, mammals, birds, reptiles, amphibians, fish, butterflies and damselflies— many of which are found nowhere else. There are some species of primitive flowering trees of the genus *Myristica* that are endemic to the region. Trees of this group give us nutmeg and mace—two valuable spices.

14. a. Mulberry

15. d. Karnataka
The Appiko movement, a radical campaign for environmental conservation, started in September 1983 and gave rise to renewed awareness about this issue throughout south India. The movement, that includes afforestation projects in barren areas, undertakes marches in the forests, educative presentations, folk performances and more. The local Kannada term for 'hugging' is 'appiko'.

16. d. Indian Mahogany

17. c. Montane grasslands interspersed with evergreen forests

18. a. Mutualism

The fig tree and the fig wasp cannot do without each other. The tiny female wasp is born and grows inside the fig. Once she matures, she mates with a male that was also born there. The male is flightless and can never leave. After breeding with the female, he chews a hole in the fig to allow her to escape. Besides breeding, this is his only job—after this, he dies. The female leaves her birth fig and, carrying pollen, flies off in search of another fig tree to pollinate and lay her eggs in. The journey can be dangerous for this tiny animal. She is guided to the new tree by chemicals that the receiving tree releases to signal its readiness for pollination. The female then enters a fig of this tree through a minute opening, lays her eggs and also pollinates the tree. And this cycle goes on. Each kind of fig tree has its own specialized pollinating wasp.

19. d. All of these

20. c. Dye

21. b. Pine Needles

22. b. Sumatra and Borneo

23. d. Lantana

Lantana is an aromatic shrub native to Central and South America. It is famous as being one of the 100 worst invasive species of the world, and has degraded and destroyed thousands of hectares of native plants. Because of its attractive flowers, it was introduced in India possibly around 1800, as an ornamental and hedge plant, by the East India Company. Since then, it has adapted and spread to almost all parts of the country, and efforts to get rid of it have failed. Today, research is being conducted on how best to manage and use the weed.

24. b. Velcro

Nature has inspired humans for centuries—in art, literature and in the great scientific inventions that are so important to us today. George de Mestral studied a simple bur, a type of seed, and invented the method of using hooks and loops for fasteners. It started after a hunting trip in the Alps. De Mestral noticed these burs clinging to his dog's fur and his own clothes. When he looked at them under a microscope, he saw that the burs were covered with hundreds of minuscule hooks that caught on to anything with a looped structure—like clothing and animal fur. After much trial and error, he came up with two nylon strips—one with loops and one with hooks. He named his invention Velcro.

25. b. Wood Apple Tree or Stone Apple Tree

Bael is one of the most utilized as well as one of the most sacred trees of India. This fruiting deciduous tree has sweet-smelling flowers, and belongs to the same family as the orange and lemon. The shell of the fruit is hard and woody, while the edible pulp inside has a sweet-and-sour taste. It has many medicinal uses, including antibiotic and anti-inflammatory properties, and is also prescribed for dysentery and other digestive problems. Sir George Watt, a well-known botanist and professor at Calcutta University, wrote in 1889, 'No drug has been longer and better known nor more appreciated by the inhabitants of India than the bael fruit.'

26. d. Growing plants in a nutrient solution without soil

27. c. Gulmohar

This flowering plant is native to the forests of Madagascar but has been introduced into several subtropical and tropical regions around the world.

28. c. Wheat

29. d. Oil Palm

Elaeis guineensis is the African Oil Palm tree species that has taken over the habitat of the orangutan in Malaysia and Borneo. Palm oil, which is made from the pulp of the fruit of the oil palm tree, is in great demand for human use in many countries, especially in India. Escalating worldwide demand for palm oil has led to the deforestation of large tracts of virgin tropical rainforests for the cultivation of oil palms.

30. d. Deodar

31. d. Xerophyte

Xerophytic plants can survive in habitats with little water, such as desert areas or snow-covered regions.

32. a. Drumstick Tree

The Drumstick Tree or Moringa is a very valuable tree that is native to India. Results of research by different agencies in several parts of the world, including India, the US Department of Agriculture (USDA), Senegal and Nicaragua—where millions of people suffer from the lack of nutritious food—show that the cultivation of the Moringa tree is extremely important due to the many uses of its leaves and pods. High in protein, calcium, vitamin C and other nutrients, they can be used to improve human health, including that of infants. It can also be used as fodder for cattle. Juice from the leaves and pods can be sprayed on young plants to improve their growth. The tree is also being used in experiments to produce biogas. In India, research on the Moringa is being conducted by the National Institute of Nutrition (NIN) in Hyderabad. Further studies are required so that each one of us can benefit from growing and using this wonder tree.

33. b. Keratin

34. b. Water Hyacinth

The Water Hyacinth is a beautiful aquatic plant, with large purple or lavender flowers. It originally grew in waterbodies of South America, possibly in the Amazon

Basin and the Brazilian Pantanal wetlands. Introduced into new areas as an ornamental water plant, it is now one of the 100 worst invasive plants in the world and has spread to North America, Africa, Asia, Australia and New Zealand. It adapts and reproduces very quickly, choking waterways as well as killing native plants, fish and other aquatic fauna, by obstructing sunlight and hindering oxygenation. This has a chain reaction, affecting water birds, other animals and humans.

35. d. All of these

36. b. Cacti

37. b. Teak

38. c. Jharkhand

39. b. Fungi

40. b. Sal

The Sal is a tropical, deciduous-forest tree of India, found in the Himalayan foothills, central and east India, and in some parts of the Deccan Plateau. It is a very valuable hard-wood timber tree, and its wood is used in construction. Sal forests were heavily exploited by the British in India, for and in the construction of railway sleepers. The leaves of the Sal are dried and used to make plates and bowls. While this is a useful tree for tribal people living in the forest, over-exploitation of the leaves harms the tree and the overall biodiversity in the long run.

41. **d. Blight**

42. **c. Giant Sequoia**
The Giant Sequoia or the Giant Redwood Tree is a coniferous species found in North America. In terms of bulk, it's the largest tree species with only one trunk, unlike the Banyan, which can also grow to a very large size but develops multiple trunks over a period of time.

43. **c. Indian Devil Tree**

44. **c. Bamboo**

45. **b. Mexico**

46. **d. Asparagus**

47. **c. Cyanobacteria and Fungi**
Lichens are living organisms that look like a plant, but are neither a plant nor an animal. A lichen is a combination of fungi and a type of bacteria also known as blue-green algae. Since they don't have roots, they don't extract any nutrition from the host plant they grow on, they are also self-sufficient in that they are able to produce their own food through photosynthesis. They can be very pretty and delicate to look at but, over time, are capable of splitting the rocks on which they grow. Lichens help in the formation of new soil by doing this.

48. **c. Maize**

49. **b.** **Lichens**

50. **b.** **Madhya Pradesh**

51. **a.** **Topsoil**

52.

Lotus	Karnataka
Palash	Madhya Pradesh
Pot Marigold	Bihar
Lady's Slipper Orchid	Arunachal Pradesh
Water Lily	Andhra Pradesh

53. **Rhododendron**

54. **Cashew Tree**

55. **Brazil**

Brazil is the fifth-largest country in the world, and has the richest biodiversity. With over 50 per cent of its land still under forest cover, Brazil has several different types of ecosystems—such as the Amazon Rainforest, the Atlantic Forest, the Pantanal and the Pampas. Sadly, Brazil also once had the highest rate of deforestation in the world which endangered its unique flora and fauna, such as jaguars, sloths, bush dogs, giant otters, tamarins, macaws and toucans, amongst others. Large tracts of forests are still being destroyed by cattle-ranch owners and coffee planters.

AQUATIC FAUNA

Life began in our oceans and aquatic fauna, such as molluscs, marine arthropods, corals and other invertebrates, first appeared in the Cambrian Period. Bony fish with pectoral and pelvic fins evolved thereafter, followed by amphibians—making the transition from water to land. The earth's diverse aquatic fauna includes primitive creatures like sea cucumbers and Coelacanths, as well as reptiles and—wonder of wonders—mammals too! What secrets do the oceans reveal? Is this evolution going backwards?

Not only did seafarers use the ocean to transport themselves to distant corners of the world, they also exploited its bounty to nourish themselves on the way. Today, fisheries—marine and freshwater—provide food and livelihood to millions of people living in coastal areas or around waterbodies. However, overharvesting of aquatic resources has threatened many species with extinction. Unsustainable exploitation damages the delicate aquatic food chain, and poisoning of our water sources is causing untold damage to the ecosystem.

Questions

1 Excessive nitrogen in water can cause algal blooms, which reduce oxygen, and eventually lead to diseases and the death of fish. Which aquatic animals have been used to rectify this form of nitrogen pollution caused by humans?

a. Eels   **b.** Sharks

c. Oysters   **d.** Corals

2 Which of these fishes is born gender-neutral, then turns into a male and can later turn into the dominant female?

a. Clownfish

b. King Dory

c. Painted Maskray

d. Mud Sunfish

In this instance, plastic has protected a marine animal. The sea sponge was previously over-harvested for use as padding, water filters and bathing sponges. Today, the easy availability of cheaper synthetic sponges has saved this harmless animal.

3 A human heart has four chambers. How many chambers does a fish heart have?

a. One
b. Two
c. Three
d. Four

4 Although sea anemones shelter some fish, these beautiful sea creatures are predators and feed on other fish, mussels and plankton. Which fish do they shelter?

a. Parrotfish
b. Starfish
c. Stonefish
d. Clownfish

5 Anadromous fish are born in fresh water, usually live in salt water, but return to fresh water to lay their eggs. Which of these fishes is anadromous?

a. Tuna
b. Salmon
c. Trout
d. Clownfish

6 At around 552 inches, the Whale Shark is the largest shark species in the world. What is the approximate size of the Dwarf Lantern Shark, which is the smallest?

a. 6 in.
b. 36 in.
c. 60 in.
d. 166 in.

Have you heard of the rare deep-water shark
discovered accidentally in 1976? The huge creature
had got entangled in the anchor of a US naval
research vessel in Hawaii. Seeing its enormous size,
its cavernous mouth and its thick rubbery lips, the
researchers knew immediately that this creature—
the Megamouth Shark—was very different from
other sharks, and a new discovery.

7 Rediscovered in 1938, this rare fish is a living fossil—
its closest relative exists only in fossilized remains
from the Late Cretaceous Period. Which fish is this?

   a. Coelacanth
   b. Burbot
   c. Great White Shark
   d. Anglerfish

8 Dangerous to humans, which of these is a highly
venomous sea snail species?

   a. Geography Cone
   b. Striated Cone
   c. Cloth of Gold Cone
   d. All of these

The Glory of India is a rare and beautiful sea cone;
the buying and selling of the shells of this animal is
banned in India.

9 Do you know which of these fishes uses its fins to walk on land and can also breathe through its skin?

a. Flying Fish

b. Coelacanth

c. Mudskipper

d. Butterflyfish

10 Which of these marine animals' egg-case is also commonly known as the Mermaid's Purse?

a. Skate

b. Dolphin

c. Seahorse

d. Starfish

In mythology, the Chimaera is a mysterious fire-breathing creature resembling a lion, a goat and a dragon in parts—but in ichthyology, it is a group of fish with a skeleton made of cartilage.

11 Which of these is an aquatic drifting animal in its larval stage but, as an adult, anchors itself to something solid and cannot move around on its own, becoming sessile?

a. Stone Fish

b. Giant Clam

c. Starfish

d. Sea Urchin

12 Which marine habitat has the greatest variety of species?

a. Shorelines

b. Coral Reefs

c. Marine Trenches

d. Seagrass Beds

13 What is the soft, muscular part of the snail called? This helps it to move forward by contracting and expanding.

a. Foot

b. Lobe

c. Fin

d. Slime

14 Found in the Kali River, along the Indo-Nepal border, which kind of carnivorous fish is the Goonch?

a. Catfish

b. Bull Shark

c. Trout

d. Pirhana

15 Some species of ovoviviparous sharks practise intrauterine cannibalism i.e., they eat their unborn siblings while inside the uterus. Which of these sharks does this?

a. Great White Shark

b. Sand Tiger Shark

c. Bull Shark

d. Hammerhead Shark

Have you read about sea animals like whales and sharks having a large disc-shaped wound on their bodies? This is the work of the Cookiecutter Shark (*Isistius brasiliensis*)—it scoops out a cookie-sized bite of flesh from much larger animals, and then swims away to enjoy its meal. Look up this strange creature!

16 In early times, certain tribes from the Pacific Islands used the dried skin of which marine animal as war helmets?

a. Lionfish
b. Sea Urchin
c. Porcupine Fish
d. Brain Coral

17 Which of the following type of fishes is known to feed on mosquito larvae and has been introduced in various countries to control mosquito-borne diseases?

a. Lionfish
b. Gambusia
c. Rainbow Trout
d. Torpedo Barb

18 The largest coral reef in the world is found in the Coral Sea. Of which ocean is the Coral Sea a part?

a. Arctic Ocean
b. Pacific Ocean
c. Atlantic Ocean
d. Indian Ocean

19 Which of the following is not a cetacean?

a. Whale Shark   **b.** Common Dolphin

c. Blue Whale   **d.** Dugong

20 Prepared as an expensive, and sometimes toxic, Japanese delicacy, 'Fugu' is Japanese for which fish?

a. Pufferfish

b. Barracuda

c. Stonefish

d. Lionfish

A Sea Gherkin feeds itself by collecting food on its sticky tentacles, which it then stuffs into its mouth—just like a naughty child sucking on his honey-covered fingers!

21 Which species of freshwater shark is native to India?

a. Indus River Shark

b. Ganges Shark

c. Yamuna Shark

d. Chambal Shark

22 The cowry, used as money in many parts of the world up to the 19th century, is the common name of which kind of mollusc?

a. Oyster   **b.** Cuttlefish

c. Sea Snail   **d.** Scallop

23 The sea anemone protects the clownfish from predators; the clownfish keeps the anemone clean. What is this kind of relationship called?

a. Parasitic
b. Cannibalistic
c. Mutualistic
d. Pessimistic

24 In which kind of habitat would you find a creature called a Sand Dollar?

a. River Bank
b. Swamp
c. Mud Flats
d. Marine Habitat

25 The butterflyfish, found in coral reefs, is the state animal of which union territory of India?

a. Pondicherry
b. Lakshadweep
c. Goa
d. Daman and Diu

26 26. Sea cucumbers breathe through their _____.

a. Gills
b. Nose
c. Anus
d. Skin

27 Which aquatic animal is capable of generating powerful electric shocks of up to 600 volts, which it uses for hunting, self-defence and for communicating with fellow-fish?

28 People kill around 100 million sharks every year. Many fishermen practise shark-finning—the fins are chopped off and the live sharks are thrown back into the sea to drown. What is the shark's fin mainly used for?

Fish is an important food source in many parts of India. In the Garhwal Himalayas, many Indigenous Traditional Knowledge (ITK) methods of fishing have been recorded. One of these is the use of plants which are toxic to fish. The plants, crushed and thrown into slow-flowing or dammed waterbodies, act as fish poison. Chemicals in the plant stun the fish, which then float to the surface and are easily collected by the fishers. However, this is a very wasteful fishing method, as not only are other animals harmed by the poison, but it also kills the baby fishes which are too small to eat.

29 Which is the world's largest cold-blooded animal?

30 Which marine animal without a backbone i.e., an invertebrate, has a beak and arms, and is considered to be highly intelligent?

Have you heard of the rare *Grimpoteuthis bathynectes*, nicknamed the Dumbo Octopus? Its fins, located

above its eyes look like the large flapping ears of Disney's Dumbo, the flying elephant. The octopus uses these fins to 'fly' though the water. Wouldn't you like to watch the underwater dance of the Dumbo Octopus?

31 Endemic to the Western Ghats and threatened by the illegal trade for aquarium fish, what is the common name for the fish popularly known as Miss Kerala?

32 Named after a striking African herbivore, what is the common name of this small fish from the minnow family, found in streams of the Eastern Himalayas?

33 Its babies come out fully developed from the male animal's pouch. Which aquatic animal is this?

34 What is a group of fish called?

35 What is the Latin word for 'fish'?

Answers

1. **c. Oysters**

   Studies by scientists and economic environmentalists, in Sweden and in the US, have used bivalve shellfish like oysters and mussels to remove excess nitrogen—usually created by deposits of washing soap, fertilizers and human waste—from water. This reduces the chances of harmful algal blooms (HAB). While some amount of algae in water is needed for nutrition, too much of it will cause eutrophication i.e., the removal of oxygen from water. Eutrophication leads to the death of water plants and animals. Cultivation of these shellfish has shown a reduction of aquatic nitrogen formation. Oyster reefs can also restock overfished areas, provide a source of food for people, and improve the general quality of water.

2. **a. Clownfish**

   Clownfish—like Nemo, the colourful character in the Disney animated film, *Finding Nemo*—are born neither male nor female. So young Nemo develops into a male in his early years but, as he grows bigger and older, he *could* become female and the leader of the group. The biggest clownfish becomes the dominant female, who breeds with the group's next biggest fish—the dominant male. The rest of the younger fish remain male. If the female dies, then the largest male will take her place by turning into a female and becoming the leader, while the next largest male in line will mate with her. This is how the cycle goes on.

3.   **b. Two**
Fish are ancient animals and first existed as invertebrates. Vertebrate fish evolved later and dominated the seas during the Devonian Period, also known as the Age of Fishes. After this, some fish, that had developed four limbs as well as lungs, invaded land. These were the first tetrapods, from which amphibians, reptiles, birds and mammals, including humans, have descended.

4.   **d. Clownfish**

5.   **b. Salmon**
Most kinds of salmon are born in fresh water but migrate to the ocean as adults. The wild female salmon lays her eggs, which are fertilized by the male in the nest she makes, in the gravelly bed of a clean, fast-flowing river or mountain stream. After this, the adult salmon usually die. The young spend the first few years of their

lives in fresh water, but later develop the ability to live in salt water. They mature in the sea and when they are ready to breed, they find their way to the mountain stream where they had been born. At this time, they can be seen leaping up waterfalls to reach the cold mountain waters where they'd started their lives. As they swim upstream, they provide an important source of food to fishing grizzly bears, beavers and other natural predators. The survivors proceed to reproduce and then die. Huge seafaring commercial vessels catch tonnes of these fish for humans each year, causing overfishing of the wild ocean salmon—this causes fewer numbers to return to their mountain homes, leading to food shortage for the bears and other animals that lie in wait for them. Additionally, many of the returning fish face the high walls of huge river-dams across which none of them is able to jump and reach upstream. With their path blocked, the fish population is drastically reduced and the whole chain is disrupted.

6. **a. 6 inches**

7. **a. Coelacanth**

A routine check of the leftover catch of a fishing trawler, near the mouth of the River Chalumna in South Africa, by the naturalist Marjorie Courtenay-Latimer, led to one of the most exciting zoological discoveries of the 20th century. Curator of a small museum in east London, Marjorie was sifting through various sea animals in the trawl nets on 22 December 1938, when she spotted a huge, beautiful creature—a metallic-blue fish with white spots, about 5 ft. long. She realized immediately' that it was something special, and took it back to the museum. She sent drawings of the fish to a famous ichthyologist, Professor James Smith, for identification. He was stunned to learn of the live capture of this living fossil that had lived 200 million years ago and was known only by way of 60 million-year-old fossils. He named the creature *Latimeria chalumnae*, after the young woman who had discovered it and the river-mouth where it was found. Although Smith advertised a reward of 100 pounds for further discoveries of the Coelacanth, the next modern specimen was found only after another fourteen years.

8. d. All of these

All cone snails are predators and use their venom to stun their prey which they can then capture easily. Some, in particular, are also capable of stinging humans and causing considerable harm—even death. The toxin in their venom, conotoxin, is being used in biomedical research. Today, several species of these molluscs are part of the billion-dollar illegal wildlife trade. Although protected by law in India, they are collected and sold to collectors who prize them for their beautifully shaped and intricately patterned shells.

9. c. Mudskipper

10. a. Skate

The egg-case of a skate is a brown, leathery, rectangular, pouch-shaped case, almost flat in structure and with curved horn-like projections from the four corners. The curved horns help to anchor them to seaweed or other oceanic plants. They are sometimes found washed up on the beach.

11. b. Giant Clam

12. b. Coral Reefs

13. a. Foot

14. a. Catfish

15. b. Sand Tiger Shark

In the natural world, it is indeed survival of the fittest. The Sand Tiger Shark is ovoviviparous—its embryos develop from eggs that hatch inside the body of the female and survive for some time on the egg yolk, before being born. Even while inside the womb, the embryos compete to survive. The fastest developing and strongest embryo eats its own siblings to get more nourishment and reduce competition before birth. This form of intrauterine cannibalism is called embryophagy. A female shark could have about fifty embryos inside her and sometimes only one or two will survive, after having eaten the others.

16. c. Porcupine Fish

17. **b. Gambusia**

18. **b. Pacific Ocean**

19. **a. Whale Shark**

20. **a. Pufferfish**

21. **b. Ganges Shark**

22. **c. Sea Snail**

The cowry shell is the home of the humble sea snail, and long before paper money came into vogue, this was used as currency. The shells are displayed in several museums all over the world. Shell money was commonly used in almost all continents and many countries, including India, Nepal and parts of Africa. Cowrie shells, including those of the Money Cowry (*Monetaria moneta*), are small, shiny, oval-shaped shells, which are durable and easy to handle. They have also been discovered at many archaeological sites. The word 'cowry' comes from Sanskrit and Hindi.

23. **c. Mutualistic**

24. **d. Marine Habitat**

The Common Sand Dollar (*Echinarachnius parma*) is a flattened, burrowing sea animal, whose body is covered with spines like a sea urchin. Children, who often find its bleached disc-like skeleton buried in the sand along the seashore, believe it to be mermaid money.

25. b. Lakshadweep

26. c. Anus

Most sea cucumbers are scavengers living on the ocean floor, and many of them resemble the vegetable in shape—hence the name. In India, they are endangered and have the same level of protection as the tiger since they too are listed under Schedule I of the Wildlife (Protection) Act, 1972. However, they are still illegally hunted for export and, each year, enforcement officers seize several tonnes of sea cucumbers being smuggled to China and Southeast Asia. Many species of this animal are threatened by extinction since they are popular as an expensive seafood item, and are also used in traditional oriental medicine. They are in high demand in several countries, including China. In some countries, sea cucumbers are being farmed to meet the growing demand.

27. Electric Eel

28. For Shark-fin Soup

Indonesia and India are both major catchers of sharks in the world. Top predators of the ocean, sharks are hunted for their fins, meat, liver, skin and cartilage. However, the most valuable part of the shark is its fins. Shark-fin soup is considered a great delicacy by the Chinese, served all over the world, and especially served at all events, like weddings and lavish parties. Today, with the Chinese population growing richer, more of them can afford expensive items like this soup. Many species of sharks are, therefore, severely endangered. It is a commonly known fact, that each year, more sharks are killed by people than people killed by sharks.

29. Whale Shark

30. Octopus

Cephalopods, like squid and octopus, have a parrot-like beak at the centre-point of their eight arms. The beak, made of chitin, is the only hard part in the otherwise soft body of these invertebrates, and is indigestible by most predators. Beaks of the Giant Squid have been found in the abdomen of whales and also embedded in ambergris, which is ejected by whales along with faecal matter.

31. Denison Barb or Red-line Torpedo Barb

32. Zebrafish

The Zebrafish is an omnivorous freshwater fish that lives in shoals. It mostly lives in streams, canals, ponds and flooded paddy fields. It is a blue-black fish with iridescent, silver, horizontal stripes; its beauty and its graceful body make it attractive to aquarium owners. The Zebrafish is overexploited for the commercial aquarium trade, and numbers in the wild are reducing.

33. Seahorse

The female seahorse squirts her eggs into the male's egg pouch in the front of its body. The eggs—sometimes up to 1500 in number, depending on the species—are incubated in this safe and oxygenated environment until they hatch. With the egg-pouch full, the male's abdominal area swells up. The babies emerge as tiny replicas of the adults, and have to fend for themselves.

34. School

35. Pisces

Pisces is also one of the twelve astrological signs.

ARTHROPODS AND ANNELIDS

Fossils of segmented worms, known as annelids, have been found to date back to the early Cambrian Period. These fossils are fairly rare since these invertebrates are soft-bodied and do not have skeletons. This large phylum includes aquatic and terrestrial worms, as well as leeches. An important part of the food chain and well-known for its soil-enriching activities, the earthworm is one of the most useful annelids.

Invertebrates like arthropods, on the other hand, have external skeletons, segmented bodies and legs characterized by joints. Early arthropods evolved in the sea and fossilized remains from the Ordovician Period show that they were found in great diversity during this time. This phylum includes arachnids like spiders and scorpions, insects like cockroaches, beetles, bees and butterflies, myriapods like centipedes and millipedes, and crustaceans like lobsters, shrimps and barnacles. Many arthropods are important pollinators.

Questions

1 Which body part of an earthworm is similar to the one that is found in birds?

   a. Skeleton

   b. Eyes

   c. Mouth

   d. Gizzard

2 The queen ant can produce both fertilized and unfertilized eggs. Unfertilized eggs develop into winged workers, whose only job is to fertilize the queen. What is this kind of asexual reproduction known as?

   a. Parthenogenesis   **b.** Symbiosis

   c. Natural   **d.** Binary Fission

The Indian Stick Insect is a popular children's pet in Europe and America; millions have also been kept and studied in laboratories all over the world. The female Indian Stick Insect can reproduce without a male.

3 Which of these is not an insect?

   a. Butterfly   **b.** Dung Beetle

   c. Cockroach   **d.** Spider

4 The larvae of which of these species of moths are steamed to death to obtain silk?

a. *Bombyx mori* **b.** *Antheraea frithi*

c. *Philosamia ricini* **d.** All of these

5 Female mosquitoes feed on nectar for energy. They also drink blood as they need protein for _____.

a. Strong Bones **b.** Egg Development

c. Growing Wings **d.** Good Eyesight

6 Where is the endangered Giant Gippsland Earthworm found? Its average size is about a metre.

a. Asia **b.** South America

c. Australia **d.** North America

7 Why does a ready-to-breed female dung beetle bury a ball of dung?

a. To clean the area

b. To increase soil fertility

c. To lay her egg in it

d. To attract a mate

The Japanese Beetle, native to east Asia, is a notoriously invasive species that attacks food plants in a number of countries, especially in North America.

8 The world's largest hornet, the _____ is native to the Indian subcontinent and delivers one of the most painful insect bites, which can be fatal even to humans.

a. Black-bellied Hornet
b. Oriental Hornet
c. Asian Giant Hornet
d. Greater Banded Hornet

9 Earthworm casts, or castings, contain many tiny organisms and soil nutrients. What are worm casts?

a. Earthworm Excreta   b. Earthworm Food
c. Earthworm Tunnels   d. Earthworm Eggs

10 An ant farm, primarily used for the study of ant colonies and their behaviour, is also called the

_____.

a. Aviary
b. Apiary
c. Terrarium
d. Formicarium

11 Derived from the Latin word for 'egg', an 'ootheca', meaning egg-case, is made by which of these animals?

a. Butterfly   b. Cockroach
c. Earthworm   d. Scorpion

Queen Alexandra's Birdwing, the largest butterfly in the world, is dependent on a particular

species of vine on which it feeds and lays its egg.
This is another one of the rare species whose habitat
and food source are threatened by the growing
palm oil industry.

12 Among which of these animals does the male die
soon after mating with the female?
a. Army Ant   b. Honeybee
c. Black Widow Spider   d. All of these

13 One of these insects, sacred to ancient Egyptians,
has its image carved in the temple of the Sun God at
Karnak. Which one is it?
a. Scarab Beetle   b. Honeybee
c. Queen Butterfly   d. Housefly

14 To encourage people of all ages to learn more about
insects, which country celebrates National Insect
Week once every two years?
a. India
b. United Kingdom
c. Brazil
d. Indonesia

15 Approximately, how many different types of ants are
found in the world?
a. Around 12,000   b. Around 1200
c. Around 120   d. Around 12

Have you ever seen ant eggs? They are white and look like grains of rice. Fresh ant eggs are a popular food item in Southeast Asia.

16 Some animals make temperature-controlled homes from soil, saliva and dung. They also maintain gardens inside their nests. Which insect is being referred to?

a. Moth   b. Spider

c. Bee   d. Termite

17 Which arthropod has a section of its brain in the abdominal part of its body, and can survive for as long as a week even after its head is cut off?

a. Butterfly

b. Hornet

c. Scorpion

d. Cockroach

A unique orchid, the Christmas Star Orchid (*Angraecum sesquipedale*), discovered in Madagascar, stores its nectar about 12 inches deep inside the flower. After its discovery, Charles Darwin, in 1862, predicted the discovery of an insect with an equally long proboscis, that must pollinate this flower. Twenty-one years after Darwin's death, such an insect—a moth— was actually found in Madagascar! This is a celebrated proof of his theory of evolution and co-evolution.

18 What does a bee communicate to the others in the hive when it performs the waggle dance?

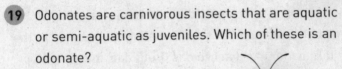

   a. Aggression

   b. Food Location

   c. Courtship Behavior

   d. Maternal Behavior

19 Odonates are carnivorous insects that are aquatic or semi-aquatic as juveniles. Which of these is an odonate?

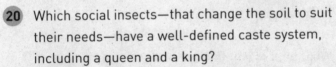

   a. Spider

   b. Praying Mantis

   c. Antlion

   d. Dragonfly

20 Which social insects—that change the soil to suit their needs—have a well-defined caste system, including a queen and a king?

   a. Ants   **b.** Termites

   c. Earthworms   **d.** Honeybees

21 What is the common term for the aerial dispersal technique used by spiders, thought to help them colonize remote, and otherwise inaccessible, islands?

   a. Gliding   **b.** Paragliding

   c. Ballooning   **d.** Windsurfing

Rare arachnids, like the Gooty Tarantula, found in India, are transported every day to different parts of the world for the pet trade by reputed courier companies. Wouldn't it be great if we could convince them to stop this? Can you come up with a plan for it?

22 A common species in India, its venom is used to create antivenin for scorpion stings. It belongs to the largest family of scorpions, Buthidae, and is one of the twenty-five scorpions whose venom is deadly to humans. What is this scorpion's common name?

23 Relative to its weight, which is the strongest living animal in the world? It can lift 1141 times its own body weight.

24 What kind of animals are ticks?

25 It can grow over a metre or 3 ft. long and can weigh about 4 kg— more than the average weight of a newborn human. What is this rare crab, found in the Andaman and Nicobar Islands, called?

'If we and the rest of the backboned animals were to disappear overnight, the rest of the world would get on pretty well. But if they were to

disappear, the land's ecosystems would collapse. The soil would lose its fertility. Many of the plants would no longer be pollinated. Lots of animals, amphibians, reptiles, birds, mammals would have nothing to eat. And our fields and pastures would be covered with dung and carrion. These small creatures are within a few inches of our feet, wherever we go on land—but often, they're disregarded. We would do very well to remember them.'

David Attenborough on invertebrates, *Life in the Undergrowth* (2005)

26 Which animal vomits its stomach's contents on to food to dissolve it so that it's easier to consume, and also lays its eggs on the food?

27 In 2014, seven species of giant pill millipedes were discovered in Madagascar. What kind of characteristic sound can these millipedes make?

28 Austrian ethologist and Nobel Laureate, Karl von Frisch, was one of the first scientists to translate the meaning of the waggle dance performed by bees. What does an ethologist study?

The use of the strands of silk-yarn, from the cocoon of the Mulberry Moth (*Bombyx mori*), was first started in China, as far back as in 2600 BC. China guarded the secret of domesticating and farming wild moths for centuries, and merchants grew rich from its exports to other countries. Silk was a valuable fibre, and the luxury fabric was used mainly by the nobility. Eventually, silk moth eggs were smuggled out of China—legends say that they were hidden in hollow bamboos—and the world discovered the secret of silk-making.

29 Adult scorpions can be of various colours, such as black, blue-black, beige, rust and brown. However, what colour are all newborn scorpion babies?

30 Which large, hairy spider is a popular pet in Europe and America? Many of its species live in silk-lined burrows underground.

Did you know that one species of spiders, *Stegodyphus lineatus*, makes the ultimate sacrifice for her babies? She stays in her burrow till her spiderlings hatch and then allows them to eat her body so that they grow strong. This cannibalistic practice is known as matriphagy.

Answers

1. **d. Gizzard**

   The gizzard is part of the earthworm's digestive system. Earthworms eat soil and soil matter, but do not have teeth. They store grains of sand and particles of rocks in their gizzard. With the help of the muscular walls of the gizzard and these particles, they mix and grind their food into a thick paste. This mixture then passes from the gizzard to the intestine. Like the earthworm, birds also lack teeth, and use their gizzards and gizzard stones similarly.

2. **a. Parthenogenesis**

3. **d. Spider**

   Spiders, scorpions, ticks and mites are arachnids.

4. **d. All of these**

   Silk is a natural fibre, made of the protein secreted by the silkworm. Sericulture, the commercial farming of silkworms for the fibre, is the basis of a multibillion-dollar luxury-fabric industry. India is one of the leading producers and consumers of silk. Millions of silk moth pupae are put to death for this demand—the moth's larvae are boiled or steamed to death to obtain the silk filament. However, for people who want to use silk that has been obtained ethically, an alternative is now available. It is called Ahimsa silk—the fabric of peace; it is only after the moth has emerged from the cocoon that the silk filament is removed for spinning and weaving.

5. b. Egg Development

6. c. Australia

The Giant Gippsland Earthworm *(Megascolides australis)*, a huge, endangered earthworm species—sometimes over 2 m long—is found only in small patches in Australia. When it was first discovered in the 1870s, it was mistaken for a snake. However, Professor Frederick McCoy, the then director of the Museum for Natural History, in Victoria, identified and described it as a new species of earthworm. It lives mostly underground near waterbodies, and eats organic matter, such as plant roots. Most of its forest habitat has been destroyed in order to create grazing land for sheep and cattle. In Australia, it is against the law to capture or keep this earthworm without permission.

7. c. To lay her egg in it

Dung beetle is the common name for a number of beetles of different families, most of which feed either partly or wholly on droppings of different mammals. Some species of the dung beetle roll a ball of dung and pull it into a burrow just below the dung pile, while others roll it away to an underground hole nearby. Some beetles feed on the dung pellets, while others lay a single egg in the dung ball. After the larva hatches, it can feed on the dung and grow. A few well-recognized dung beetles are the Egyptian Scarab Beetle, the Goliath Beetle, the Rhinoceros Beetle and the Japanese Beetle.

8. **c. Asian Giant Hornet**

9. **a. Earthworm Excreta**

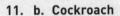

10. **d. Formicarium**

11. **b. Cockroach**
An ootheca is the hardened egg-sac of a cockroach, which may contain up to fifty eggs. Some cockroaches carry their ootheca around with them until the eggs hatch.

12. **d. All of these**

13. **a. Scarab Beetle**
The Egyptian Scarab Beetle (*Scarabaeus sacer*) was considered to be a manifestation of Ra, the Sun God, and was revered in ancient Egyptian culture.

14. **b. United Kingdom**
Since insects play such a valuable role in the ecosystem but do not get the recognition that they deserve, the Royal

Entomological Society, founded in 1833, celebrates the week-long event in the month of June, once every two years. In 2016, National Insect Week was celebrated from 20 to 26 June.

15. a. Around 12,000

16. d. Termite

Termite mounds—some of them up to 9 m high—are one of the most impressive homes constructed by an animal. Built with termite saliva, soil and dung—the walls of these structures are porous, and the upper storey has a network of tunnels that lead to a central chimney. Air is constantly circulated through these ducts and pores, keeping the termite-home cool and oxygenated. This ensures that ideal conditions are maintained for living and food storage. The controlled temperature is also perfect for the termites' fungus 'garden', which is located in the main nest area below the ground.

17. d. Cockroach

18. b. Food Location

19. d. Dragonfly

20. b. Termites

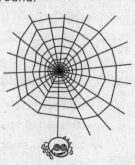

21. c. Ballooning

Studies indicate that ballooning is mostly performed by juvenile spiders. The spider climbs to a high spot and releases multiple silk threads into the air, which catch the breeze and lift the spider off the ground. A ballooning spider can travel a few metres or even hundreds of kilometers to reach new habitats. Sometimes, ballooning spiders who land on water can also survive.

22. **Indian Red Scorpion**

23. **Dung Beetle**

24. **Ticks are parasitic animals that live and feed on the bodies of other animals**

25. **Coconut Crab**
This is one of the largest species of arthropods that lives mainly on land. It's related to hermit crabs and, like others of this family, lives inside a shell for protection. However, it does this only when it's young and relatively small; the Coconut Crab abandons its shell later in life when its body and skin toughen, and it grows quite large. It's found on islands in the Pacific and Indian Oceans, usually where one would find Coconut Palm Trees. It has large and powerful pincers that it uses to remove the husk from the coconut and get to the sweet flesh inside. People who harvest coconuts consider the Coconut Crab a robber. It's eaten in many parts of the world and is becoming increasingly rare. In India, it's protected under the Wildlife (Protection) Act.

26. **Bluebottle Fly (*Calliphora vomitoria*)**
Larger than the Housefly, the Bluebottle is easily recognized by its metallic-blue colour and red eyes.

They usually lay their eggs in rotting carcasses or open wounds, so that the maggots that hatch there have an easily available food source and can grow rapidly.

27. **They can chirp**

28. **Animal Behaviour**

29. **White**

30. **Tarantula**

Tarantulas are massive venomous spiders that are large and hairy, and mostly live underground. Various species are found in different parts of the world, such as Central and South America, parts of southern Europe, Africa, Asia and Australia. They are carnivorous and bear fangs that are attached to their venom ducts; these help the spiders subdue their prey. They eat insects, frogs, lizards and, sometimes, even small birds. Since they are attractively coloured and their venom is not normally harmful to humans, many are hunted for the pet trade. Tarantulas have special detachable hair on their abdomen, which are released when the spider is threatened—this can irritate the skin terribly. The Goliath Bird-eating Spider, a species of tarantulas, is found in parts of South America and is one of the largest spiders in the world.

AMPHIBIANS AND REPTILES

Ancient amphibians evolved from bony four-limbed fish when the ocean levels were high and the earth was relatively warm. Shifting from life in the ocean to a life that is semi-aquatic and terrestrial, amphibious tetrapods dominated the land during the Carboniferous Period. The word 'amphibian' is derived from the Greek word 'amphibios' which refers to their dual life. Amphibians need water to lay their eggs in, since the eggs lack protective shells. They usually start life as aquatic larvae, and develop lungs as they mature so that they can lead a more terrestrial existence. Sensitive to water, soil and air quality—biologists use them as an early warning system of environmental change.

Prehistoric reptiles evolved from early amphibians during the Carboniferous Period, and the group diversified during the Permian Period. Early reptiles proliferated mainly because they were amniotes i.e., they laid eggs with outer membranes, and therefore didn't need to reproduce in water. This enabled most reptiles in shifting from a semi-aquatic status to a terrestrial one.

Questions

1 Once plentiful, this species was hunted to extinction for its meat, and Lonesome George was the last of his subspecies when he died in 2012 at around 100 years of age. To which species did he belong?

a. Olive Ridley Turtle   **b.** Galapagos Giant Tortoise

c. Komodo Dragon   **d.** Gila Monster

> One of the six species of caimans found in the world today, the Spectacled Caiman has a good tolerance for salt water, and is hunted for its skin. It's named so as it has large eyes with lighter-coloured bony rims around them that look like spectacle frames!

2 Why are cat snakes so called?

a. They eat cats   **b.** They have whiskers

c. They have eyes like cats   **d.** They hiss like cats

> All reptiles—even though they may spend a lot of time in water—come ashore to lay their eggs.

3 Which of these reptiles can focus both its eyes separately to look at two different objects at the same time?

a. Iguana   **b.** Chameleon

c. Tuatara   **d.** Thorny Devil

4 What type of animal is a Mudpuppy?

   a. Lizard

   b. Frog

   c. Caecilian

   d. Salamander

5 Who is called the Frogman of India?

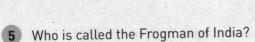

   a. Dr Anwaruddin Choudhury

   b. Dr Salim Ali

   c. Dr Sultan Ahmed Ismail

   d. Dr S.D. Biju

Some people—as Bill Haast, founder of the Miami Serpentarium Laboratories used to—take big risks by injecting themselves with small doses of snake venom to build up resistance to it. They believe that this will protect them in case they are bitten by a venomous snake.

6 The Government of Madhya Pradesh plans to denotify or withdraw protection from parts of two wildlife sanctuaries, and allow sand mining. Since animals do not recognize such boundaries, which Critically Endangered species, found only in India, is likely to suffer because of disturbance to its habitat?

   a. Olive Ridley Turtle   **b.** Sand Boa

   c. Monitor Lizard   **d.** Gharial

Scientists have published several research papers that suggest that the Indian Star Tortoise has a shell with a self-righting shape, that resembles the gömböc—a three-dimensional semi-spherical object with only one stable position of rest.

7 The birds of Guam had no experience or fear of this invasive animal, introduced to the island by humans in the 1940s, which eventually caused the extinction of around nine native birds. Which animal is this?
   a. Cane Toad
   b. Water Monitor
   c. King Cobra
   d. Brown Tree Snake

8 Which of these snakes has adapted to digging?
   a. Cobra   **b.** Pit Viper
   c. Shieldtail   **d.** Cat Snake

9 What is the term used for a group of turtles?
   a. Bunch   **b.** Box
   c. Bale   **d.** Brood

10 The study of frogs informs us about changes in the ecosystem, therefore they are known as _____.
   a. Indicator Species   **b.** Umbrella Species
   c. Flagship Species   **d.** Invasive Species

11 Rarer than the Bengal Tiger, under which Schedule of the Indian Wildlife (Protection) Act, 1972 is the Gharial protected?

a. Schedule I

b. Schedule II

c. Schedule IV

d. Schedule V

Did you know that crocodiles and alligators have vertical pupils like those of a cat?

12 Primarily where in India does the world's largest sea turtle, the Leatherback, nest?

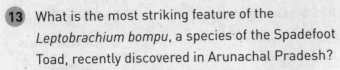

a. Tamil Nadu

b. Lakshadweep

c. Kerala

d. Andaman and Nicobar Islands

13 What is the most striking feature of the *Leptobrachium bompu*, a species of the Spadefoot Toad, recently discovered in Arunachal Pradesh?

a. Highly venomous

b. Blue-and-green striped skin

c. Blue-grey eyes

d. All of these

14 The closest living relatives of the Indian Purple Frog—which is a rare, recently discovered species—are found on the _____.

a. Seychelle Islands   **b.** Andaman Islands

c. Komodo Island   **d.** Lakshadweep Islands

15 Turtles are hunted for the yellowish cartilaginous substance found next to their lower shells; it's considered a delicacy in Southeast Asian soups. What is it called?

a. Carapace   **b.** Calipee

c. Plastron   **d.** Scutes

16 The harmless Kingsnake imitates the bright red, yellow and black bands of the venomous coral snakes as a defence against predation. What form of mimicry is this?

a. Müllerian Mimicry

b. Batesian Mimicry

c. Aggressive Mimicry

d. Automimicry

'Red touches yellow, kills a fellow.
Red touches black, venom lack.'

This is a rhyme that children in North America
learn so that they can tell the venomous Coral
Snake from the harmless Kingsnake. The

rhyme describes the order of the red, black and yellow bands on the snake's skin. Usually, very colourful snakes are dangerous, but sometimes a harmless one imitates a dangerous one for self-defence and survival!

17 Who is the film-maker and producer of the film, *The Ridley's Last Stand*, an award-winning film about the life and survival of the Olive Ridley Sea Turtles that nest along the Orissa coast?

a. Kartick Shanker
b. Krishnendu Bose
c. Shekar Dattatri
d. Kartick Satyanarayan

18 In J.K. Rowling's Harry Potter books, Draco is the name of Harry's school rival. In zoology, which of these animals belongs to the genus *Draco*?

a. Flying Frogs
b. Flying Snakes
c. Flying Lizard
d. Flying Turtle

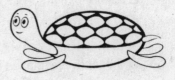

19 Poison Dart Frog is the common name for a group of frogs found in Central and South America. These amphibians are named so because they _____.

a. Shoot poisonous darts as a form of defence
b. Have bright dart-shaped patterns on their skin
c. Secrete poison in which natives dip their darts
d. All of these

20 Which of these snakes does not belong to the genus *Naja* and is not a true cobra?

a. Spectacled Cobra

b. Central Asian Cobra

c. Samar Cobra

d. King Cobra

Because of their unique flora and fauna, the Galapagos Islands were declared a national park, and are also a UNESCO World Heritage Site.

21 *Snakeman: The Story of a Naturalist* by Zai Whitaker is the story of which herpetologist, otherwise affectionately called 'Pambukaran'?

a. Romulus Whitaker

b. Sathyabhama Das Biju

c. Gerry Martin

d. J.C. Daniel

22 Which of these snakes is a burrower, with a head and tail so similar in appearance, that it is often mistakenly thought as having two heads?

a. Sand Boa

b. Vine Snake

c. Rat Snake

d. Russell's Viper

23 Which live animals are injected with snake venom to produce antivenin or antivenom at the Haffkine Institute, Maharashtra?

a. Dogs
b. Gorillas
c. Horses
d. Rats

> Beware—you could easily mistake the highly dangerous Saw-scaled Viper (*Echis carinatus*) for the harmless Cat Snake (*Boiga trigonata*) as both look very similar. The good news is that if bitten, you can quickly take the antivenom injection at the nearest hospital!

24 Which kind of tracking device is used in India to monitor migrating sea turtles?

a. Radio Collar
b. Acoustic Tag
c. Coded Wire Tag
d. Platform Terminal Transmitter

25 What is the estimated population of the Gharial left in the wild?

a. 1500–1800   b. 200–500
c. 750–850   d. 2000–2300

26 Which venomous Indian snake when alarmed, coils its body and rubs its rough scales together to produce a distinct warning sound?

  a. Rattlesnake
  b. Saw-scaled Viper
  c. Russell's Viper
  d. King Cobra

27 Which country has no wild snakes?

  a. Scotland   **b.** Ireland
  c. Sweden   **d.** Germany

28 Adwaita lived for over 200 years and died in 2006 at the Alipore Zoological Gardens, Kolkata. What species of tortoise was he?

  a. Aldabra Giant Tortoise
  b. Galapagos Giant Tortoise
  c. Star Tortoise
  d. Travancore Tortoise

The tortoise, with its protective shell—into which it can withdraw its legs and head—was the inspiration for the Roman war formation called the testudo formation, 'testudo' being the Latin word for 'tortoise'. In this strategy, soldiers, marching in rows, aligned their shields to protect themselves from all sides, including the top—just like the sides and the top of the box-like tortoiseshell.

**They could then march forward without any fear
of the enemy's arrows and spears. Wasn't that
clever of the Romans?**

29 Which part of a turtle is the carapace?

   a. Top Shell

   b. Bottom Shell

   c. Meat

   d. Cartilage

30 How many species of sea turtles are there
worldwide?

   a. Seven   **b.** Nine

   c. Twelve   **d.** Fifteen

31 Pit vipers use their loreal pits—deep depressions
on either side of their head—to detect prey
through _____.

   a. Sound   **b.** Smell

   c. Infrared   **d.** Taste

32 According to the Species Survival Network (SSN),
which of these freshwater turtles is most commonly
hunted for the commercial sale of its meat?

   a. Star Tortoise

   b. Southeast Asian Softshell Turtle

   c. Leatherback Turtle

   d. Loggerhead Turtle

Fossilized remains of the largest land tortoise that ever lived, *Megalochelys atlas*, have been found in the Sivalik Hills of north India. It lived millions of years ago in western India and Pakistan.

33 Which part of the Olive Ridley Turtle's life cycle is commonly referred to as the 'lost years', since sightings of the turtle are very rare during this period?
a. Nesting and hatching
b. First three to seven years
c. Breeding years
d. Old age

34 After mating in offshore waters, female sea turtles come ashore and dig a _____ -shaped nest in the sand.
a. Cup
b. Tunnel
c. Flask
d. Mound

35 The Turtle Excluder Device (TED) allows turtles to escape from the nets of commercial trawlers, that fish off the coast of Orissa, with a minimum loss of the intended catch. What is the main catch targeted by these trawlers?
a. Dolphins
b. Prawns
c. Trout
d. Mackerel

Of the three Indian Crocodilian species, the Indian Saltwater Crocodile is the only one that

makes a mound nest of earth, leaves and other vegetation, with the eggs laid in a depression on top of this mound and then covered up. The other two—the Marsh Crocodile and the Gharial—both dig hole nests in sandy banks, lay their eggs and then cover them up.

36 Which of these Indian snakes kills by constriction?

a. King Cobra   **b.** Vine Snake

c. Rat Snake   **d.** Rock Python

37 Match the species with the locations where they are found:

Olive Ridley	Agumbe Rainforest
Gharial	Gahirmatha Marine Sanctuary
King Cobra	Idukki District
Pig-nosed Frog	Bhitarkanika National Park
Saltwater Crocodile	National Chambal Sanctuary

The Russell's Viper, one of India's most venomous snakes, was named after Patrick Russell—a well-known naturalist of the East India Company—who wrote *An Account of Indian Serpents, Collected on the Coast of Coromandel* (1796).

38 Match these rare reptiles and amphibians with their home countries:

Purple Frog	Mexico
Komodo Dragon	Guyana
Matamata	Montserrat
Mountain Chicken	India
Axolotl	Indonesia

39 It's quite normal to spot a crocodile sleeping with its mouth wide open. Why do they exhibit this peculiar behaviour?

When people are said to shed crocodile tears, it means that they are pretending to be sad when they are actually not. Crocodiles really do shed tears—but not because they are sad. Their eyes tear up when they are out of water, so that they remain clean and moist.

40 What is the common name for the lizard, *Sitana ponticeriana*. It's associated with a character from Hindu mythology?

41 The rare Pig-nosed Frog is native to India and spends most of its life underground. It surfaces only for a short period of time to mate and reproduce in ponds, ditches and streams. During which season does this occur?

42 What is another common name for the Indian Marsh Crocodile?

43 The Texas Horned Lizard lives in desert areas and rests in burrows in the soil. Besides effective camouflaging, what is its other unique method of defence in case of an attack?

While there are about twenty-three different species of crocodilians found worldwide—including alligators, caimans, crocodiles and the Gharial— there are around 6500 different species of lizards, such as chameleons, geckos, iguanas and monitors.

44 What is the particular branch of zoology that is the specialized study of amphibians?

The Sidewinder Rattlesnake has protrusions or 'horns' above its eyes that are thought to protect them from sand while digging.

45 In the Harry Potter universe, the Basilisk was a serpent. What kind of animal is it in the natural world?

> **Did you know that Master Oogway, the senior Kung Fu Master in the animated film-series, *Kung Fu Panda*, was a Galapagos Giant Tortoise?**

46 What is the most important factor that decides whether a sea-turtle egg will hatch into a female or a male turtle?

> **Bull alligators use infrasound to attract females; they vibrate the midsection of their bodies underwater, with their heads and tails raised in a kind of inverted arch. The infrasound causes the water around them to vibrate and bubble. The result is the water-dance of alligators—a fascinating mating ritual!**

47 What is one of the Leatherback Turtle's favourite prey species, despite it being extremely venomous?

48 Among which animal population is Chytridiomycosis, a deadly fungal disease, currently causing a mass decline?

49 Why is the Green Sea Turtle so named?

50 Is a Marsh Crocodile's snout shaped like an 'A' or 'U'?

The Indian Spiny-tailed Lizard lives in burrows, in arid regions of Rajasthan and Gujarat. Although protected by the Wildlife (Protection) Act, 1972, it is poached in large numbers. In India, the lizard is boiled to extract its oil, which is said to have medicinal properties.

Answers

1. **b. Galapagos Giant Tortoise**

   Lonesome George, a Pinta Island Tortoise—a subspecies of the Galapagos Tortoise, hatched on a sandy beach of Pinta Island, the northernmost of the Galapagos Islands. The only remaining one of his kind, he was discovered by a scientist in 1971 and taken to the Charles Darwin Research Station (CDRS) on Santa Cruz Island. Many attempts were made to find him a suitable mate, of his own subspecies or from related subspecies, but without success. Famous all over the world, Lonesome George died in 2012 without producing any offspring. He was estimated to be 100 years old at the time of his death.

2. **c. They have eyes like cats**

   Cat snakes belong to the group of snakes called *Boiga*, and are mainly nocturnal; they live in trees, shrubs and bushes. They have large eyes with cat-like vertical pupils. Cat snakes reproduce by laying eggs and they feed on lizards, frogs, small rodents and birds. Although slightly venomous, they are usually not harmful to humans.

However, people kill them often as they can be mistaken for vipers due to the triangular shape of the head.

3. **b. Chameleon**

4. **d. Salamander**
   Salamanders are amphibians that resemble lizards, and can be either aquatic or terrestrial as adults. The Mudpuppy (*Necturus maculosus*) is found in North America, and is mainly nocturnal and aquatic. Like most other amphibians, they need a moist habitat; they are carnivorous and feed on small animals like worms, snails and insects. Salamanders are known for their ability to regenerate their limbs.

5. **d. Dr S.D. Biju**
   Professor Sathyabhama Das Biju, a conservation biologist and a taxonomist, is one of the most famous amphibian experts in India. He heads the Systematics Lab at the University of Delhi, Department of Environmental Studies, and is also Project Head for the exciting LOST! Amphibians of India (LAI) project. Along with his team of researchers, Dr Biju has discovered several new species of frogs in different parts of the country.

6. **d. Gharial**
   Sand, a valuable natural resource, is extracted from ocean beds, riverbeds, beaches and deserts. Mixed in with other materials to create cement, it is mined for its minerals as well as for its use as building material in the lucrative real

estate business all over the world. Poorly managed sand mining causes damage to the environment as well as impacts wildlife. In India, sand mining is banned in most national parks and sanctuaries—but being controlled by the powerful mining mafia, it often continues illegally. Several government staff have lost their lives upon coming in conflict with these influential people. In 2015, the government of Madhya Pradesh announced a plan to denotify or withdraw protection from some wildlife habitats in order to legalize sand mining in the area. These areas are currently part of the National Chambal Sanctuary and the Son Gharial Sanctuary, which are two of the remaining habitats of the Gharial. Human activities, like sand mining and agriculture on the riverbanks, disturb the Gharial's nesting habitats and that of several endangered species of freshwater turtles.

7. **d. Brown Tree Snake**

A type of cat snake, the Brown Tree Snake is native to Papua New Guinea. It was accidentally introduced by way of a cargo shipment to the island of Guam—a territory of the United States in the Pacific Ocean. It is listed by the IUCN in its Global Invasive Species Database as one of the 100 worst invasive species in the world. It has caused the extinction of most of the endemic island birds and lizards, thereby affecting the biodiversity of the ecosystem. Since there were very few predators of the snake on the island, and there was abundant prey for it, the snake multiplied quickly. Besides being a formidable predator, it has also caused huge financial losses by getting into power substations and causing power outages. The US has tried all sorts of methods to get rid of the snakes—snake traps, sniffer dogs, snake hunters and inspectors—but they continue to overrun the island, and attempts to remove them is proving to be time-consuming and costly. The US Government has conducted a study that involves airdropping poisoned mice on the island in a new attempt to kill the invaders.

8. c. Shieldtail

9. c. Bale
There are other collective nouns used for turtles as well—such as nest, turn or dole.

10. a. Indicator Species

11. a. Schedule I
India's Wildlife (Protection) Act was passed by Parliament in 1972 to protect India's plant, animal and wildlife habitats. Plants and animals are protected under six Schedules, each with different levels of protection as well as penalties upon violation. Species listed under Schedule I and Schedule II Part ii enjoy absolute protection. The tiger and the Gharial are both Schedule I species. The clauses of the Act aren't set in stone and

are altered from time to time; the changes that are made in the Wildlife Act are called Amendments.

12. d. Andaman and Nicobar Islands

13. c. Blue-grey eyes
This species is new to scientific study, and was only described in 2011. The frogs were discovered in the Eaglenest Wildlife Sanctuary, a biodiversity hotspot, hidden in leaf litter near a stream.

14. a. Seychelle Islands

15. b. Calipee

16. b. Batesian Mimicry
Named after the naturalist Henry Walter Bates, this is a method of adaptation for survival, wherein a harmless species imitates the use of warning-signals otherwise used by a dangerous one. These signals include the display of bright, eye-catching colouration and patterns. The harmless species fools predators into thinking that it's dangerous, so that they leave it alone.

17. c. Shekar Dattatri

18. c. Flying Lizard
Draco is the Greek word for dragon, and is the name given to the genus of flying lizards that are found in South and Southeast Asia. These lizards cannot actually fly, but glide from tree to tree using a thin flap of skin that expands when needed. There are about forty recognized

species; out of those, one—the Southern Flying Lizard—is found only in India, mainly in the Western Ghats. The Blandford's Flying Lizard is found in India, Bangladesh and other neighbouring parts of Southeast Asia. Like most other lizards, they are non-venomous and pose no harm to people.

19. c. Secrete poison in which natives dip their darts

20. d. King Cobra
The King Cobra (*Ophiophagus hannah*) is from the family of elapids, which are venomous snakes with characteristically hollow fangs. Their fangs are connected to venom glands, which are located towards the back of their mouths. The King Cobra is the only species of the genus *Ophiophagus*.

21. a. Romulus Whitaker

22. a. Sand Boa

23. c. Horses
Usually, horses are used by the Haffkine Institute to produce the antidote for snakebites. Snakes are 'milked' for their venom which is then freeze-dried. Small doses of the snake venom, which are not fatal to the horse, are injected into the animal so that their bodies produce antibodies that fight the venom. These antibodies are extracted from the horse, processed and used to produce the antivenin that saves millions of human lives each year.

24. d. Platform Terminal Transmitter

Satellite tracking, or telemetry, is used to follow the paths of migratory marine animals, like sea turtles, who are international travellers and swim great distances across the world's oceans. A Platform Terminal Transmitter (PTT) is a device with an antenna that is attached to the turtle's back. Each PTT has a unique number; it sends signals with the turtle's location and other important information to a satellite each time the turtle comes up to the sea surface to breathe. Since sea turtles breathe air, they have to resurface several times a day. This data is then downloaded on to the researchers' computer, which reveals essential facts about these animals, including where and when the females come to shore to lay their eggs and where they go after that.

25. c. 750–850

26. b. Saw-scaled Viper

27. b. Ireland

28. a. Aldabra Giant Tortoise

The Aldabra Tortoise is named after the Aldabra Atoll in Seychelles. The species is also found in Madagascar and Tanzania. Although it is the animal with the longest natural lifespan, sailors have hunted these giant tortoises—for easy meat—to the point of extinction. It is said that Adwaita, who was housed at the the Alipore

Zoological Gardens in Kolkata, was brought by sailors, from the Seychelle Islands, as a gift to Major-General Robert Clive of the East India Company.

29. **a. Top Shell**

30. **a. Seven**
The seven species of sea turtles that are found in the world's oceans are the Leatherback, the Loggerhead, the Green, the Hawksbill, the Olive Ridley, the Kemp's Ridley and the Flatback Turtle. Of these, the first five are found in Indian waters.

31. **c. Infrared**

32. **b. Southeast Asian Softshell Turtle**

33. **b. First three to seven years**

34. **c. Flask**

35. **b. Prawns**
Commercial mechanized prawn-fishing vessels, known as trawlers, use a dragnet with fine mesh to catch shrimp, prawns and fish for the fisheries industry. Bottom trawling, which disturbs the seabed, is damaging to the marine environment. Additional harm to the ecosystem is caused due to by-catch of non-target species like dolphins, sharks and sea turtles that also get caught and die. Like humans, sea turtles use their lungs to breathe and drown when they are trapped in the trawl nets. A

net fitted with a Turtle Excluder Device allows turtles and larger animals to escape from a special opening in the middle of the net, while retaining most of the prawns. A small amount of the catch can also escape, but this is a relatively small loss. Unfortunately, implementing the use of TEDs on commercial fishing vessels is a problem and turtles, even in the breeding season, continue to die in this way.

36. d. Rock Python

All pythons are constrictors i.e., they kill their prey by suffocation. Being ambush hunters, who catch their prey by surprise attacks, they are more active at night and feed mainly on warm-blooded animals. Three species of pythons are found in India and all are protected. Pythons are hunted for their valuable skin and meat, and to be kept as pets.

37.

Olive Ridley	Gahirmatha Marine Sanctuary
Gharial	National Chambal Sanctuary
King Cobra	Agumbe Rainforest
Pig-nosed Frog	Idukki District
Saltwater Crocodile	Bhitarkanika National Park

38.

Purple Frog	India
Komodo Dragon	Indonesia
Matamata	Guyana
Mountain Chicken	Montserrat
Axolotl	Mexico

39. **To cool off and maintain body temperature**

40. **Sita's Lizard or Fan-throated Lizard**

41. **Monsoon**

42. **Mugger**

43. **It squirts blood from its eyes when disturbed**

    The state reptile of Texas, USA, the Texas Horned Lizard looks like a miniature dinosaur with a collar of spikes around its neck and along its back. Its colouration blends perfectly with its desert habitat. When threatened, the lizard puffs itself up to appear larger in order to scare predators away. If neither of these techniques work, it uses its unique ability to squirt a jet of blood from its eyes, aimed at the predator.

44. **Batrachology**

45. **Lizard**

    The Basilisk is a kind of lizard that belongs to the genus *Basiliscus*. They are found in Mexico, Central America and the northern part of South America. They are known for their ability to run on their hind legs in an upright position. While escaping from predators, they have been seen sprinting across the surface of water too—this has earned them the name, Jesus Christ Lizard.

46. **Temperature**

    The female turtle comes to the shore when she is ready to lay her eggs. She digs a nest pit above the high-tide line, about 1 m deep, and deposits about twenty-five to 150 eggs in it. After covering the pit with sand, she returns to the ocean—leaving the sun and the sand to incubate her eggs. The temperature at which the eggs are incubated determines whether they hatch into male or female turtles. Different species have different temperature levels for males and females. In some sea turtles, for example, eggs that hatch at above 29°C are females, while males develop at slightly lower temperatures. A balance of males and females is maintained by earlier and later nesting within the season.

47. Box Jellyfish

48. Frogs

49. Because of its green-coloured fat
Protected under the Wildlife (Protection) Act, 1972, this turtle is not named after the colour of its shell or skin, as it's commonly believed to be. It is, in fact, named after the greenish colour of its fat.

50. 'A'
Unlike alligators, who have wide and rounded U-shaped snouts, the Mugger has a pointed A-shaped snout.

MAMMALS

Fossils of jaw bones and teeth indicate that early mammals evolved around 200 to 250 million years ago, in the Triassic Period. The first true mammals can be assumed as being tiny shrew-like animals that probably had a diet that largely consisted of insects. Today, the class Mammalia includes animals that are warm-blooded, have body hair, possess mammary glands and usually give birth to live young. Many have highly developed brains.

Rodents are the largest group of mammals and the smallest group is that of the monotremes—mammals who reproduce by laying eggs.

Today, the IUCN has classified around thirty mammalian species as Critically Endangered (Possibly Extinct) (CR[PE]) and the Living Planet Index (LPI) shows a 39 per cent decline in all terrestrial animal species, with an overall drop of over 50 per cent among all vertebrates, between 1970 and 2010.

Questions

1. Which two national parks in India have all five of these threatened megafauna—tiger, leopard, elephant, rhinoceros, and Swamp Deer?
   a. Kanha and Corbett
   b. Sundarbans and Dudhwa
   c. Dudhwa and Kaziranga
   d. Nagarhole and Corbett

2. A mass of tissue, located in their foreheads, helps dolphins with communication and echolocation. What is this mass called?
   a. Jacobson's Organ
   b. Melon
   c. Beak
   d. Blowhole

3. Which one of these species of macaques, found in India, was sent into outer space? It was one of the first non-human primates to return alive.
   a. Rhesus
   b. Pig-tailed
   c. Bonnet
   d. Lion-tailed

Naruto, a Celebes Crested Macaque, was involved in a legal battle over selfies that she took herself in

2011. Naruto took a series of selfies with a camera that belonged to David Slater, a wildlife photographer. Slater later published these in a book which made them both famous. The People for Ethical Treatment of Animals (PETA) said that Naruto, not Slater, was the copyright holder and rightful owner of her selfies. The matter was taken to court—who do you think won? And who do you think is the rightful owner of the selfies?

4 Mammals of the order Lagomorpha, like hares and rabbits, are herbivores and have four incisors in their top jaw. Which of these animals is also a lagomorph?
- **a.** Squirrel
- **b.** Shrew
- **c.** Pika
- **d.** Marmot

5 A tapir—found in Central America, South America and Southeast Asia—looks like a large pig with a short trunk. To which of these pairs of animals is it genetically related?
- **a.** Elephant and Hippopotamus
- **b.** Pig and Elephant
- **c.** Rhinoceros and Horse
- **d.** Pig and Rhinoceros

6 We humans have seven vertebrae in our necks. How many vertebrae does a giraffe have in its neck?

a. Seven
b. Eleven
c. Fifteen
d. Nineteen

7 Gerald Durrell, the famous conservationist, wrote many books, such as *My Family and Other Animals* and *The Aye-aye and I*. What kind of animal is the Aye-aye?

a. Mongoose
b. Bat
c. Hyena
d. Lemur

Have any of you been to the Andaman Islands and met Rajan, the celebrity elephant? Rajan is a famous ocean-swimming Asiatic Elephant and has even starred in the Hollywood film, *The Fall*. Visitors to the island have had the unique experience of diving and snorkelling in the crystal-clear waters with this magnificent tusker.

8 Machli the tigress is famous for having been given the Travel Operators for Tigers (TOFT) Lifetime Achievement Award, for her contribution to conservation and the tiger-tourism economy. To which tiger reserve does Machli belong?

a. Bannerghatta
b. Ranthambore
c. Corbett
d. Sundarbans

9 Some whales feed with the help of baleen plates that act as strainers in their mouth. What is baleen made of?

a. Dentine

b. Keratin

c. Cartilage

d. Bone

10 Which of these is the largest kind of dolphin?

a. Killer Whale

b. Whale Shark

c. Ganga River Dolphin

d. Bottlenose Dolphin

11 On which mammal was Master Shifu, from the Kung Fu Panda films, modelled?

a. Red Fox

b. Red Panda

c. Honey Badger

d. Lemur

12 Which warm-blooded animal has the largest and heaviest brain?

a. Whale Shark

b. Elephant

c. Hippopotamus

d. Sperm Whale

13 Which of these mammals has teeth that never stop growing?

a. Porcupine

b. Wild Ass

c. Mongoose

d. Rhinoceros

14 Which charismatic animal is the international symbol for the wildlife conservation movement?

   a. Bengal Tiger   **b.** Giant Panda

   c. Dodo   **d.** Peacock

> Suraj the one-eared elephant was saved from a shackled existence as a temple elephant in Maharashtra. Kept in chains, he rarely saw sunshine. Luckily for Suraj, he was rescued and, after travelling 1500 km by road, he arrived safely on Christmas Day 2015 at the Wildlife SOS Rescue Centre. It is sad that although elephants are worshipped in India, many of them suffer in captivity, at the hands of man. Now Suraj, at the age of forty-five, has a changed life.

15 The Rhesus Macaque is common in north India. Which macaque is common in south India?

   a. Stump-tailed   **b.** Lion-tailed

   c. Bonnet   **d.** Crab-eating

16 Based on their genus, which of these wild cats is the odd one out?

   a. Bengal Tiger   **b.** Asiatic Lion

   c. Clouded Leopard   **d.** Common Leopard

17 In terms of size, which of these is the world's smallest mammal?

   a. Bumblebee Bat   **b.** Mole Rat

   c. Vaquita   **d.** Dormouse

18 Which species of ungulates—hoofed mammals—has an alarm call that sounds like a dog barking?
   a. Sambar
   b. Kakar
   c. Chital
   d. Sangai

19 Today, most wild horses are actually feral—descendants of escaped domesticated horses. Which of these is the only remaining true wild horse in the world?
   a. Tarpan
   b. Mustang
   c. New Forest Pony
   d. Przewalski's Horse

20 Of the twenty-nine states and seven union territories in India, how many have tigers?
   a. Nine
   b. Thirteen
   c. Eighteen
   d. Twenty-one

Although tigers are found in south India and are strong swimmers, there are no tigers in Sri Lanka.

21 She made important discoveries about the communication, diet and social relationships of gorillas. Who is this famous conservationist, based on whose life the Hollywood film, *Gorillas in the Mist* (1988), was made?
   a. Jane Goodall
   b. Rachel Carson
   c. Anne Wright
   d. Dian Fossey

22 Approximately how many species of mammals exist on earth today?

a. 1500–2500

b. 5000–6000

c. 15,500–16,500

d. 25,000–26,000

23 What is the tail fin of a whale called?

a. Pectoral

b. Dorsal

c. Pelvic

d. Fluke

24 Among these herbivores, all except one are mainly grazers. Which one of these is a browser?

a. Hippopotamus

b. Dugong

c. Capybara

d. Giraffe

25 Which of these animals, also found in India, is the largest wild mountain goat species in the world?

a. Himalayan Tahr

b. Greater Blue Sheep

c. Markhor

d. Asiatic Ibex

26 What is a squirrel's nest called?

a. Sett

b. Holt

c. Drey

d. Sty

27 How many finger-like projections does the Asiatic Elephant have at the end of its trunk?

a. One

b. Two

c. Three

d. Four

It is conventionally accepted that there are two species of elephants—the African Elephant (*Loxodonta africana*) and the Asiatic Elephant (*Elephas maximus*). Hybridization is rare between the two species. One recorded hybrid at Chester Zoo, in the UK, was born by interbreeding an African male, Jumbolina, with an Asiatic female, Sheba. He had some characteristics of his African father, and some of his Asiatic mother. Sadly, however, the calf did not survive for long and died around twelve days after he was born.

28 Leopards, the most adaptable of India's 'big cats', coexist with tigers and can live in almost all types of habitats. Which tiger reserve in India has no leopards?
   a. Bandipur   **b.** Pench
   c. Dudhwa   **d.** Sundarban

29 Which of these is the largest Indian deer?
   a. Barasingha   **b.** Kashmir Red Deer
   c. Sambar   **d.** Brow-antlered Deer

30 The dominant male gorilla in a group is called a Silverback. What are the younger male gorillas, who support the leader, called?
   a. Brownbacks   **b.** Blackbacks
   c. Greybacks   **d.** Saddlebacks

31 Although not from the cat family, it has fully retractable claws and is an agile climber. Which animal is this?

a. Ratel   **b.** Red Panda

c. Spotted Linsang   **d.** Dhole

32 Some types of otters are social and live together in a small group. What is a group of otters called?

a. Colony

b. School

c. Troop

d. Raft

33 What kind of animal is Rikki-Tikki-Tavi in *The Jungle Book* (1894) by Rudyard Kipling?

a. Mongoose   **b.** Hyena

c. Civet   **d.** Wolf

34 Which of these is the world's largest arboreal—tree-dwelling—mammal?

a. Chimpanzee

b. Orangutan

c. Gorilla

d. Baboon

35 Koko is a primate who is famous for her prowess in sign language, and has also been recorded as having adopted a pet kitten. To which species does Koko belong?

a. Human **b.** Chimpanzee

c. Gorilla **d.** Bonobo

36 Which of these mammals has ossicones—antler-like protrusions covered with skin and hair—on its head?

a. Okapi **b.** Musk Deer

c. Tapir **d.** Narwhal

37 To which country is the Bonobo, human's closest relative, endemic?

a. Angola

b. Democratic Republic of Congo

c. Central African Republic

d. Nigeria

38 Which of these tiger subspecies is not extinct?

a. Caspian Tiger **b.** Javan Tiger

c. Malayan Tiger **d.** Bali Tiger

Did you know that the tiger's tongue is covered with tiny, sharp bristles, called papillae? This makes its tongue very rough, like sandpaper, and helps it to scrape the skin off its prey, as well as keep its own coat clean.

39 With a total population of around fifty individuals, which Critically Endangered leopard subspecies is found in the 'Land of the Leopard' National Park?
- **a.** Amur Leopard
- **b.** Sri Lankan Leopard
- **c.** Javan Leopard
- **d.** Indian Leopard

40 In India, we have wild hares but no wild rabbits. What is the home of a hare called?
- **a.** Burrow
- **b.** Form
- **c.** Sett
- **d.** Warren

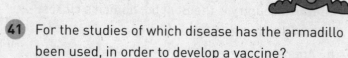

41 For the studies of which disease has the armadillo been used, in order to develop a vaccine?
- **a.** AIDS
- **b.** Tuberculosis
- **c.** Leprosy
- **d.** Hepatitis B

42 Many mammals have a vestigial digit that does not reach the ground and is not in use while they walk. What is this digit called?
- **a.** Dewclaw
- **b.** Fetlock
- **c.** Carpal pad
- **d.** All of these

43 Of great interest in evolutionary studies, which of these unique animals has the smallest number of chromosomes?
- **a.** Tibetan Antelope
- **b.** Siberian Tiger
- **c.** African Cheetah
- **d.** Indian Muntjac

44 The Dugong, found in the Andaman and Nicobar Islands and the Laccadive Islands, is a marine mammal on the brink of extinction in India. What is its favourite food?

  a. Sea Snail
  b. Fish
  c. Seagrass
  d. Krill

The extent of a tiger's territory also depends on how much prey is available. A male tiger's territory is larger than the female's, and overlaps that of several females.

45 How many countries have adopted the tiger as their national animal?

  a. Three   **b.** Four
  c. Five   **d.** Six

46 In the German fairy tale, 'Snow White', by the Brothers Grimm, the wicked queen commands the huntsman to kill Snow White and return with her liver and heart as proof. In the story, with which animal's organs does the huntsman actually return?

  a. Deer
  b. Wild Boar
  c. Hare
  d. Wolf

47 Elephants communicate by making long-distance infrasonic sounds, which are inaudible to humans. What is this sound called?

a. Trumpet

b. Squeal

c. Rumble

d. Roar

The Indri, or Babakoto as it is called in Malagasy, is considered to be the largest species of living lemurs. It eats mainly leaves but also seeds, fruits and flowers. Although it is well-known for its striking black and white colouration, some Indri can have a dark coat all over.

48 Which of these is a baleen whale and not a toothed whale?

a. Right Whale

b. Blue Whale

c. Humpback Whale

d. All of these

49 To which group does the Chousingha, a mammal with four horns, belong?

a. Sheep

b. Goat

c. Deer

d. Antelope

50 Which of these animals assists the Indian Laburnum Tree by eating the pods, that germinate after passing through their gut?

a. Jackal

b. Civet

c. Macaque

d. All of these

51 Which mammal's cubs are born with canines and incisors already erupted?

a. African Lion

b. Bengal Tiger

c. Spotted Hyena

d. Golden Jackal

52 Which is the only country in the world where lemurs are found?

a. Tasmania

b. Brazil

c. Madagascar

d. Malaysia

53 Which of the following is the largest zoo in India, and also a conservation breeding centre for the endangered Lion-tailed Macaque?

a. Alipore Zoological Gardens

b. Arignar Anna Zoological Park

c. Sri Chamarajendra Zoological Gardens

d. Sri Venkateswara Zoological Park

54 Which of these is the largest even-toed ungulate found in peninsular India?

a. Gaur

b. Nilgai

c. Indian Rhinoceros

d. Indian Elephant

55 Which of these animals has a proboscis?

   a. Elephant

   b. Tapir

   c. Saiga Antelope

   d. All of these

You will be shocked to know that, in 1929, the sons of US President Theodore 'Teddy' Roosevelt tracked a Giant Panda in the mountains of China. They came across it sleeping peacefully. It woke up and started eating bamboo shoots. The brothers, Theodore and Kermit Roosevelt, opened fire and killed the helpless, sleepy animal on the spot. They earned the distinction of being the first Westerners to kill one of these rare and beautiful animals.

56 Which animal, sacred in Egyptian culture, used to be given an extravagant burial and was even mummified?

   a. Dog   **b.** Tiger

   c. Rat   **d.** Cat

57 Which is the rarest wild cat in the world?

   a. Snow Leopard

   b. Leopard Cat

   c. Clouded Leopard

   d. Amur Leopard

58 Which of these national parks contains the largest population of the endemic Nilgiri Tahr?

a. Periyar
b. Eravikulam
c. Mudumalai
d. Nagarhole

The Sea Mink, a large relative of the American Mink, was hunted to extinction in the second-half of the 19th century by European fur traders. Unfortunately, not very much is known about this beautiful reddish-brown mustelid since it became extinct before scientists could study and document its habits.

59 Which of these is the world's largest predator of warm-blooded animals?

a. Tiger
b. Grizzly Bear
c. Killer Whale
d. Blue Whale

60 Which of these is a non-threatening vocalization made by tigers?

a. Roar
b. Prusten
c. Snarl
d. Growl

61 Which of these is an egg-laying mammal?

a. Pangolin
b. Echidna
c. Dolphin
d. Dugong

62 Which member of the cat family cannot retract its claws fully?

a. Fishing Cat

b. Clouded Leopard

c. Caracal

d. Cheetah

Hunting large mammals in India was a popular sport even up to the 20th century. Historical records show that in Sarguja, a princely state of central India, Maharaja Ramanuj Saran Singh Deo killed at least 1100 tigers, 2000 leopards and one cheetah in his lifetime!

63 Which of these is the national aquatic animal of India?

a. Indian Smooth-coated Otter

b. Ganga River Dolphin

c. Dugong

d. Finless Porpoise

64 Which of these antelope species, protected by Indian law, did Bollywood actor Salman Khan shoot?

a. Nilgiri Tahr

b. Chital

c. Blackbuck

d. Musk Deer

65 A shoat is the young one of which animal?

a. Wild Boar

b. Dolphin

c. Gibbon

d. Stoat

66 Which mammal's habitat does the Bhimashankar Wildlife Sanctuary, in the Western Ghats, protect?

a. Great Indian Bustard **b.** Clouded Leopard
c. Indian Giant Squirrel **d.** Nilgiri Tahr

67 The loris is a small primate. How many species of lorises are found in India?

a. Two **b.** Four
c. Six **d.** Eight

68 Which physical sampling method was used to estimate the tiger population in the last all-India Tiger Census conducted in 2014?

a. Pitfall Traps **b.** Pugmark Impression Pads
c. Drones **d.** Camera Traps

69 She was hand-reared by Saroj Raj Choudhury, field director of the Simlipal Tiger Reserve. Besides humans, her playmates were Jambo the bear and Bagha the dog. Which of these books documents her life?

a. *Through the Tiger's Eyes*
b. *Tara: A Tigress*
c. *Born Free*
d. *Khairi: The Beloved Tiger*

Wild cats, like tigers and leopards, living in Jim Corbett National Park are in danger because of the

villagers' dogs. These dogs can transmit diseases, like rabies, to them—as in the case of Saroj Raj Choudhury's tigress, who died of rabies. The Humane Society International (HSI) India estimates that there are around 17,000 dogs living in the buffer zone of the national park. Most of these are not vaccinated and are a threat to both wildlife and humans.

70 In how many Indian states is the Gangetic River Dolphin found?
  a. Five   **b.** Seven
  c. Nine   **d.** Eleven

71 Which animal is mass-slaughtered for its fine downy wool, that is used to produce expensive shahtoosh shawls?
  a. Chiru   **b.** Goral
  c. Urial   **d.** Takin

72 'Tyger Tyger, burning bright,
In the forests of the night;
What immortal hand or eye,
Could frame thy fearful symmetry?'

Which poet penned this famous poem in 1794?
  a. Rudyard Kipling   **b.** Belinda Wright
  c. William Blake   **d.** Jim Corbett

Project Tiger was inaugurated on 1st April 1973 at Corbett National Park. WWF International raised one million dollars for this—a lot of it through the efforts of children, like you, in Europe. A group of twenty-seven of these children, invited to India by the Indian Government, visited the Sariska Tiger Reserve— they were thrilled to spot a tiger!

73 How many species of mammals are found in India?
- **a.** 150–250
- **b.** 350–450
- **c.** 1050–1150
- **d.** 2050–2150

74 What is a young hare called?
- **a.** Pup
- **b.** Leveret
- **c.** Whelp
- **d.** Squab

75 Which male marine mammal has a single long spiral tusk?
- **a.** Manatee
- **b.** Beluga Whale
- **c.** Walrus
- **d.** Narwhal

76 Which species of dolphin is found in Chilika Lake?
- **a.** Irrawaddy
- **b.** Gangetic
- **c.** Bottle-nosed
- **d.** Spotted

77 Where in India are Marmots, a species of large rodents, found?
   a. Kaas Plateau
   b. Nilgiri Hills
   c. Aravalli Hills
   d. Changthang Plateau

78 Which of these animals is the Okapi's closest relative?
   a. Zebra
   b. Nilgai
   c. Giraffe
   d. Tapir

79 Which of these continents is best known for the wild Dingo?
   a. Asia
   b. Australia
   c. Africa
   d. Europe

80 Which was the last species of the ape—sharing 98.7 per cent of its DNA with humans—to be discovered?
   a. Gorilla
   b. Orangutan
   c. Bonobo
   d. Gibbon

81 Which Critically Endangered leopard subspecies has the lowest level of genetic variation in the surviving population?
   a. Indian Leopard
   b. Persian Leopard
   c. Javan Leopard
   d. Amur Leopard

82 How many countries in the world today still have wild tigers?

a. Eight   b. Ten

c. Thirteen   d. Sixteen

There are more tigers kept in captivity in the US than there are wild tigers left on earth. In some parts of the United States of America, you don't even need a licence to own and keep a pet tiger in your backyard or apartment!

83 Three of these tiger subspecies are extinct and one is classified as Critically Endangered (Possibly Extinct in the Wild) (CR[PEW]) by the IUCN. Which one?

a. South China Tiger

b. Javan Tiger

c. Bali Tiger

d. Caspian Tiger

84 Declared Possibly Extinct in 1978, this mammal of the viverrid family was rediscovered in 1987. However, it has not been reported since 1990, and there are no known photographs of this animal. Which endemic Indian viverrid is this?

a. Binturong   b. Spotted Linsang

c. Malabar Civet   d. Nilgiri Marten

85 What is a labyrinth of rabbit burrows known as?
- **a.** Tunnel
- **b.** Warren
- **c.** Sett
- **d.** Form

86 Rodents need to gnaw constantly on fibrous material to wear down their continuously growing incisors. Which other group of mammals needs to do this as well?
- **a.** Mustelids
- **b.** Canids
- **c.** Lagomorphs
- **d.** Felids

87 Which of the following animals' name comes from the Greek word for 'river horse'?
- **a.** Elephant
- **b.** Rhinoceros
- **c.** Tapir
- **d.** Hippopotamus

88 Most species of male deer shed their horns seasonally. Which deer species does not?
- **a.** Spotted Deer
- **b.** Muntjac
- **c.** Red Deer
- **d.** Reindeer

One of the most dangerous animals in Indian jungles, at least for humans, is the Sloth Bear. He has poor eyesight and powerful curved claws, which make him vicious when disturbed. Kenneth Anderson wrote about a particularly aggressive bear that he shot in Mysore, in his story, 'Alum Bux and the Big Black Bear'.

89 How many fingers and modified 'thumbs' does the giant panda have in each of its front paws?
- **a.** Four fingers and no 'thumb'
- **b.** Four fingers and one 'thumb'
- **c.** Five fingers and no 'thumb'
- **d.** Five fingers and one 'thumb'

90 Bears are hunted for their gall bladders and paws. What are the paws in demand for?
- **a.** Soup
- **b.** Leather
- **c.** Ornaments
- **d.** Musical Instruments

91 In which of these Protected Areas can you find the beautiful but endangered Golden Langur?
- **a.** Jaldapara National Park
- **b.** Khangchendzonga National Park
- **c.** Dibang Wildlife Sanctuary
- **d.** Chakrashila Wildlife Sanctuary

Kenneth Anderson (1910-74), a British shikari, wrote about a langur that was killed by a Wild Dog in his story, 'What the Thunderstorm Brought':

'The langurs came down now and surrounded the carcass of their companion. Some smelled it, others handled it. An old female, who might have been its mother, picked it up and kissed it. The large black eyes in those jet black faces seemed strangely shiny and moist. Do langurs weep?'

92 Bears and humans, amongst others, are plantigrade mammals. This means that they _____.
a. Eat plants
b. Walk with their toes and heels flat on the ground
c. Do gardening
d. Communicate using loud noises

93 Which is the only country in the world where both lions and tigers are found in the wild?
a. Nepal
b. South Africa
c. India
d. Uganda

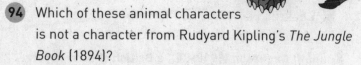

94 Which of these animal characters is not a character from Rudyard Kipling's *The Jungle Book* (1894)?
a. Akela
b. Bagheera
c. Rafiki
d. Tabaqui

95 In which part of India were elephants and Spotted Deer introduced by the British? The animals have

degraded the vegetation since and
are a threat to the fragile ecosystem.

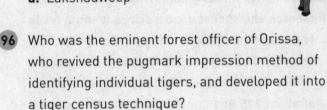

a. National Capital Region
b. Andaman and Nicobar Islands
c. Jammu and Kashmir
d. Lakshadweep

96 Who was the eminent forest officer of Orissa,
who revived the pugmark impression method of
identifying individual tigers, and developed it into
a tiger census technique?

a. Valmik Thapar   **b.** Fateh Singh Rathore
c. Saroj Raj Choudhury   **d.** Asad Rehmani

97 Which Indian state has the largest number of tiger
reserves?

a. Karnataka   **b.** Maharashtra
c. Madhya Pradesh   **d.** Tamil Nadu

98 Poached for its musk pod, the endangered Himalayan
Musk Deer has no antlers, but has a pair of tushes or
tusks which are actually elongated _____.

a. Incisors   **b.** Premolars
c. Canines   **d.** Molars

The illegal trade in wildlife is growing and is a
serious threat to wild animal populations. Some

of the items most valuable to smugglers and traders are elephant ivory, tiger parts, rhino horn, caviar, exotic birds and reptiles. Besides the direct loss of biodiversity, the trade in animals and their parts also leads to the spread of zoonotic diseases which further threaten both wildlife and humans. Research shows that unauthorized wildlife trade is linked to the illegal smuggling of drugs. In one well-known case, US Customs officials in Miami found cocaine stuffed into the bellies of about 225 Boa Constrictors. All the snakes involved died of injuries.

99 The Dugong, a marine mammal with flippers and a fluked tail, has the same level of legal protection as the tiger in India. Which of these is its closest relative?

a. Manatee   **b.** Walrus

c. Dolphin   **d.** Sea Otter

100 Which of these animal parts is traditionally used to make the charango—a musical instrument played in Ecuador, Peru, Bolivia and parts of Chile and Argentina?

a. Bison Horn   **b.** Porcupine Quills

c. Monitor Lizard Hide   **d.** Armadillo Shell

101 Match the species with the Protected Area where it is found:

Sloth Bear	Kanha National Park
Nilgiri Tahr	Vikramshila Wildlife Sanctuary
Swamp Deer	Balphakram National Park
Marbled Cat	Eravikulam National Park
Gangetic Dolphin	Daroji Wildlife Sanctuary

Reindeer have been very important to people living in the Arctic and subarctic regions. Besides being hunted for meat, they have also been domesticated— to be used as livestock and to drive sleds, as told in the popular legend of Santa Claus. They are called Caribou in North America.

102 Match the conservation biologist with their associated species:

Dr Raghu Chundawat	Tiger
Alan Rabinowitz	Snow Leopard
Gerald Durrell	Giant Panda
Dr Ullas Karanth	Aye-aye
George Schaller	Jaguar

103 Match the national animals with their respective countries:

Snow Leopard	Mexico
Jaguar	Ethiopia
Tiger	Afghanistan
Giraffe	Bangladesh
Lion	Tanzania

104 Match the baby names with the animals:

Joey	Llama
Pup	Dugong
Foal	Kangaroo
Cria	Wild Ass
Calf	Bat

**A baby kangaroo is really
tiny when it's newly born. It can be shorter
than an inch and weigh less than a gram,
even if it is the baby of the large Red Kangaroo,
that can be 6 ft. tall—as tall as a grown man.
Compare this to a human baby at birth, which is
about 14–20 in. in size. Blind and hairless,
the baby kangaroo crawls into its mother's pouch
where it feeds on milk, and continues to grow for the
next eight months.**

105 Match the animals with their animated-film characters:

Meerkat	Flower, *Bambi*
Reindeer	Akela, *The Jungle Book*
Skunk	Sven, *Frozen*
Ring-tailed Lemur	Timon, *The Lion King*
Indian Wolf	King Julian, *Madagascar*

106 Match the Indian state animals with their states:

Barasingha	Andhra Pradesh
Indian Elephant	Madhya Pradesh
Blackbuck	Kerala
Fishing Cat	Meghalaya
Clouded Leopard	West Bengal

107 What colour is the Blue Whale's faeces? It looks like a huge explosion from a paint factory.

On 11 January 2016, over eighty Pilot Whales were beached on the coast of Tuticorin in south India. Although local fishermen tried to push them back, most of the whales died.

108 The Walrus is a gigantic marine mammal with tusks, and can weigh up to 2000 kg. It is found in three of the world's oceans. The Pacific and Atlantic oceans are two of those—which is the third?

109 Like humans, they have no tails and are thought to pair for life. Which Indian ape species is this?

110 How many species of big cats are found in India? The term is used for large cats of the genus *Panthera*, which includes cats that can roar.

111 Which is the smallest of all marine mammals?

112 The orangutan's habitat is threatened by large-scale deforestation for the cultivation of palm oil—which is commonly used in ice cream, chocolates, pizzas, packaged bread, instant noodles, cookies, shampoo and cosmetics. Which country is the world's largest importer of palm oil?

113 While whale-watching, how can you tell a male Killer Whale from a female?

114 To raise awareness about the status of tigers, which day is celebrated as Global Tiger Day each year?

115 Recognized as one of the most unusual animals on earth, which primate species has unique teeth? Like those of a rodent, its incisors continue to grow throughout its life.

116 The endangered Nilgiri Langur, found only in south India, is hunted for its body parts, including its flesh and its beautiful glossy fur. What is its skin mainly used for?

117 It is scaly, protects itself by rolling into a ball and gives off a foul smell when disturbed. Which Indian mammal is this?

118 In the late 1960s, international prices of tiger skins skyrocketed. In 1969, while addressing the IUCN in Delhi, which Indian prime minister said, 'We need foreign exchange but not at the cost of the life and liberty of some of the most beautiful inhabitants of this continent'?

Early in the 1990s, a young English girl, Belinda Wright, went to a small hole-in-the-wall phone booth in Baihar, a small town near the Kanha Tiger Reserve. Here, the phone-booth owner discreetly offered to sell her four tiger skins. Passionate about wildlife conservation, Belinda reacted quickly and said that she knew someone who would be

interested in buying them. She proceeded to set up a sting operation with a fake buyer, and the man was soon arrested by the police. Belinda went on to start the Wildlife Protection Society of India (WPSI), an NGO which is involved in undercover operations for collecting information about and investigating tiger poaching cases in the country. Don't you think that's a dangerous but exciting career?

119 Which jackal species is the only one to be found outside Africa—in parts of Europe and Asia, including India?

120 To intercept poachers and traders of wildlife items, a permanent dog-squad was set up in 2015. On the very first day of duty, a sniffer dog caught a person carrying animal nails and bones. Where in India was this?

121 They are good climbers and are the most arboreal of the large Indian felids—which animal is this?

Peter Lund, the Danish naturalist, discovered fossils of a large carnivore in a limestone cave in Brazil. At first, he thought it was a hyena-like animal, but after finding foot bones and large curved fangs, he realized that it was a huge cat species. He named this prehistoric animal *Smilodon populator*, also famously known as the Sabre-toothed Cat.

122 The Gir National Park is the last stronghold of the Asiatic Lion. Which nomadic tribe do these endangered lions share their habitat with?

123 What is a specialized adaptation developed in certain primates, including lemurs, for personal grooming?

124 What is a group of Meerkats called?

125 Which species is the largest aquatic mammal found in Indian rivers?

126 What is the usual height of a newborn Giraffe?

127 Hunted for its meat, this tiny herbivore makes its den in tree hollows; it has no horns and is the smallest deer in India. Which species is this?

128 Which camel species, usually found in hot deserts, has only one hump?

129 The Scaly Anteater is a mammal with hard scales that protect it when it is attacked. What are the scales made of?

130 The One-horned Rhinoceros, the Asiatic Elephant and the Bengal Tiger are three WWF Priority Species. On which Indian banknote do all three appear?

Because its habitat is shrinking rapidly, the Indian Rhinoceros sometimes resorts to raiding farmers' crops on the fringe of the national park. They enjoy feeding on crops of hot chilli plants, but are not very fond of mustard!

131 Valuable in the high-end perfume industry, what is this element of the Sperm Whale's excreta called?

132 A sportswear company, Reebok, is named after the Grey Rhebok. What kind of animal is this?

133 Which country has the greatest species diversity on earth for non-human primates?

134 A relatively common prey species, this ungulate has a close association with the langur. It benefits from the langur's messy food habits, good eyesight and high vantage point when watching for predators. Which species is this?

135 Besides humans, which other mammal builds dams?

136 Marmots live high up in the Himalayan mountains. What kind of homes do they have?

137 Flying Foxes are megabats—the family of very large bats. What is the other common name for members of this bat family?

The Sucker-footed Bat is a rare species that is found only on the island of Madagascar. It uses its unique foot pads to stick to smooth leaf-surfaces—even when they are vertical, just as geckos can! Did you know that scientists studying these bats have found several males, but almost no females? Wouldn't you like to be the one to discover more about this strange mammal?

138 The male member in a group of Kiangs defends his territory as well as his females against rivals. What is the male Kiang known as?

139 Tigers learn survival skills from their mothers. Which Indian conservationist, who lived near the Dudhwa

National Park, experimented with releasing a hand-raised tigress back into the wild?

140 How can you tell a male Hoolock Gibbon from a female?

141 Which extinct species did Manny depict in the animated film-series, *Ice Age*?

142 Highly social, this top predator shares the habitat of tigers and leopards, and is known for its unique whistling calls. Which animal is this?

143 Which Himalayan national park is one of the few places on earth where the rare Kashmir Red Deer can be seen in the wild?

Tropical forests still hold many secrets. Did you know that only in 1999 was a wild mammal species, called Saola, photographed alive for the very first time? A picture of this shy, Critically Endangered animal was taken in a camera trap that was set up by the Vietnamese Forest Protection Department and WWF.

144 In June 2015, a 40 ft.-long female whale was washed up on the coast of Revas in Maharashtra. Although efforts were made to rescue it, it died. What kind of whale was this?

145 Famous for its massive spiralling horns, the Argali is the largest wild sheep found in India. One subspecies is named after a famous 13th-century explorer who has described this animal in his book. Who was he?

146 What is the unique feature of the Chousingha—a species now only found in India, with possibly a few remaining in Nepal?

147 Where in India is its only ape species, the Hoolock Gibbon, found?

148 Killer Whales are fearsome ocean predators with powerful jaws, yet they are very caring parents and seldom leave their babies alone. What does the mother Killer Whale feed her newborn baby?

149 What is the main difference that is immediately noticeable between a female Asiatic Elephant and a female African Elephant?

150 After a pilot project in Panna in 2014, which new technology does the National Tiger Conservation Authority (NTCA) plan to use to monitor tigers?

The tiger is revered in many cultures, including Chinese. They believe that it is a special animal as

its head is marked with the Chinese character that stands for 'king'. If you look at the pattern closely, it does look quite similar!

151 The 'songs' of this huge animal are some of the most beautiful and haunting sounds of the ocean. Which marine species is this?

152 Himalayan Marmots live at altitudes above 3500 m (above sea level) and sleep through the winter months. During this time, on what do they survive?

153 The Walrus feeds mainly on fish and shellfish. Which highly developed sensory organs help the Walrus detect prey?

154 Two-humped Camels are native to Central Asia, and a small population can be seen in the Nubra Valley. What is another common name of this species?

155 Which animal's habitat is threatened by mining for the ore called coltan? Coltan is used in a number of products, including mobile phones.

156 What does 'orang-utan' mean in Malay?

157 What is another common name for the Killer Whale?

158 Cecil, the lion, lived in the Hwange National Park and was being studied by the University of Oxford. He was lured out of the park, injured and finally shot by the American trophy hunter, Walter Palmer. From which country was Cecil?

Have you heard of 'canned hunting'?
It is the cruel sport of trophy-hunting exotic
large animals in a captive environment—sometimes
even via a webcam, with the use of a remote-
controlled gun. The poor animals, including tigers
and lions, are in confined areas with
no way of escaping.

159 Besides China, which Asian country is the largest market for pangolin derivatives, including its scales and meat?

160 Gorillas are threatened mainly by habitat loss and poaching. Which zoonotic disease is another threat to gorilla populations?

Answers

1. **c. Dudhwa and Kaziranga**

   The Dudhwa National Park is located in Uttar Pradesh, on the Nepal border, while the Kaziranga National Park is located in Assam, in Northeast India. Both parks have extensive grasslands and swampy marshes.

2. **b. Melon**

   Sound travels faster in water than in air, and both whales and dolphins use this to their advantage. Through the melon, dolphins produce high-frequency sounds, which travel long distances. This organ is mainly made up of fatty tissue and is located on the top of the head. The melon differs in size according to the species.

3. **a. Rhesus**

   Both NASA and the Soviet's space programmes have experimented with sending non-human primates, such as Rhesus Macaques and chimpanzees, to outer space. Able was the first Rhesus Macaque to return alive to earth along with Miss Baker, a squirrel monkey. Unfortunately, however, Able died soon after.

4. **c. Pika**

5. **c. Rhinoceros and Horse**

6. **a. Seven**

7. **d. Lemur**

8. **b. Ranthambore**
    Machli (code number: T-16) is one of the oldest tigresses in Ranthambore, and probably the most photographed. She was named so because of her facial markings, which are said to resemble the shape of a fish. She has earned the park fame and funds, and has starred in a number of documentary films. Famous for her fight with a large crocodile, she is skilled at killing these huge reptiles that inhabit the Raj Bagh Lake. A good provider and teacher, she has raised around nine clubs to adulthood, resulting in the increase of Ranthambore's tiger population.

9. **b. Keratin**
    Baleen whales are mostly very large in size, but feed on some of the smallest sea creatures, like krill and plankton. The Blue Whale, the planet's largest animal, is a baleen whale.

10. **a. Killer Whale**
    The male Killer Whale can be over 30 ft. long.

11. **b. Red Panda**

12. **d. Sperm Whale**

13. **a. Porcupine**

14. **b. Giant Panda**

The Giant Panda is rarely spotted in the wild and was first seen alive by a European as late as the early 20th century. The first live Giant Panda was brought from China to the US by an American fashion designer. WWF was one of the first international conservation organizations to work with the Chinese Government for the conservation of the Giant Panda in China. It became the inspiration for the well-recognized WWF logo which was created in 1961.

15. **c. Bonnet**

16. **c. Clouded Leopard**

Based on genetic analysis, the tiger, the lion, the leopard and the Snow Leopard all belong to the genus *Panthera*— the Clouded Leopard does not. All *Panthera* species, except the Snow Leopard, can roar.

17. **a. Bumblebee Bat**

It is also known as the Kitti's Hog-nosed Bat due to it's snout-like nose, and is classified as an endangered species.

18. **b. Kakar**

The Indian Muntjac or Kakar is also known as the Barking Deer because of its characteristic alarm call. It's a small and ancient species of deer.

19. d. Przewalski's Horse

20. c. Eighteen

21. d. Dian Fossey

Dr Dian Fossey studied Mountain Gorillas in the Virunga region for many years and won the trust of the gorilla group. She was particularly fond of a young male whom she'd named Digit and who was cruelly killed by poachers in the prime of his life. After his death, Dian doubled her efforts for gorilla protection and started the Digit Fund. In 1983, she published her well-known book, *Gorillas in the Mist*. Tragically, she was murdered in her cabin in the Virunga Mountains in 1985.

22. b. 5000–6000

23. d. Fluke

24. d. Giraffe

Plant-eating animals that feed mainly on grasses are known as grazers, while those that feed mainly on tree leaves are called browsers.

25. c. Markhor

A Markhor has a long, shaggy coat, a tufted beard and corkscrew horns. It is found at high altitudes in Uzbekistan, Tajikistan, Turkmenistan, Afghanistan, Pakistan and India. The horns are greatly prized by trophy hunters and, in colonial times, the British considered it to be one of the most challenging game-animals because of the inhospitable terrain in which it lives. Besides being hunted by people for meat and sport, its main predators are bears, Snow Leopards, lynx and wolves.

26. c. Drey

27. a. One

28. d. Sundarban

29. c. Sambar
An adult male can weigh up to 270 kg.

30. b. Blackbacks

31. c. Spotted Linsang

32. d. Raft

33. a. Mongoose

34. b. Orangutan

35. c. Gorilla
Koko is a Western Lowland Gorilla who is part of The Gorilla Foundation's ongoing research on interspecies communication. Dr Penny Patterson, then a PhD student at Stanford University, first taught the one-year-old Koko how to communicate using sign language, in 1972. In 1984, Koko selected and adopted a kitten who was called All Ball. The *National Geographic* magazine featured a story titled, 'Koko's Kitten', which portrayed the gorilla's gentleness towards her pet. Apple Inc. has worked with The Gorilla Foundation to give Koko a voice, using a software that can translate icons on a computer into spoken words.

36. a. Okapi

37. b. Democratic Republic of Congo

Like humans, Bonobos are from the subfamily Homininae, which also includes gorillas and chimpanzees. Bonobos are more slender and graceful than chimpanzees, and are more capable of walking on two legs—they have been seen wading upright through water, using a stick for support, much as we would. In Bonobo society, females are equal in status to the males. The intercommunication of Bonobos has been described as constant chattering and may be accompanied by gestures as well as facial expressions.

38. c. Malayan Tiger

39. a. Amur Leopard

The rare Amur Leopard, called 'Bars' in Russian, lives in the temperate forests of the Russian Far East. Habitat destruction, poaching of the leopard for its beautiful spotted coat and hunting of its prey species, threaten its survival. There may be as few as around seventy of these animals left in the wild today.

40. b. Form

41. c. Leprosy

Although leprosy, as a disease afflicting humans, has been known for the last 4000 years, it was only in 1873 that the bacterium that causes it was discovered. Since armadillos have a low body temperature that suits the growth of this bacterium, the Nine-banded Armadillo, also vulnerable to the disease, has become the main test-subject for the vaccine. Humans can also get infected from eating or handling these armadillos.

42. a. Dewclaw

Mammals, such as deer, dogs, some species of cats and many others, are digitigrades—they walk on their toes and not on their whole foot, and usually have a vestigial toe or claw i.e., a digit that grows higher up on the foot and is not used while walking. The digit usually grows on the front feet.

43. d. Indian Muntjac

44. c. Seagrass

45. c. Five

Bangladesh, India, Malaysia, Myanmar and South Korea have adopted the tiger as their national animal. Governments and NGOs all over the world have adopted TX2—the goal to double the number of tigers in the wild by the year 2022, the next Year of the Tiger. Humans are the biggest threat to tigers.

46. b. Wild Boar

47. c. Rumble

The low-frequency rumble that elephants make, by way of communicating, is difficult to analyse and study, since we cannot hear this infrasonic sound. Audio-recording collars have been used on African Elephants to study these sounds. It appears that elephants can recognize the 'voices' of herd members just as we can recognize our friends' voices without actually seeing them.

48. d. All of these
Whales and dolphins belong to the group Cetartiodactyla that includes hippopotamuses, pigs, deer, Giraffes and other hoofed mammals. There are two kinds of whales—baleen whales and toothed whales. Baleen whales, unlike toothed whales, have no teeth but have a sieve-like structure for filtering plankton instead.

49. d. Antelope

50. d. All of these

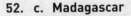

51. c. Spotted Hyena
As a survival strategy among Spotted Hyenas, the stronger cub sometimes kills the weaker one.

52. c. Madagascar

53. b. Arignar Anna Zoological Park

54. a. Gaur

55. d. All of these
A proboscis is an elongated and flexible facial appendage.

56. d. Cat
In ancient Egypt, cats were sacred and were mummified just as the pharaohs were, upon their death. The Egyptians loved their domesticated cats who would protect their grain from rats. Bastet, the cat goddess,

was associated with fertility, motherhood and the home; statues of the Bastet were common in Egyptian society.

57. d. Amur Leopard

58. b. Eravikulam

The Nilgiri Tahr is an Endangered ungulate species, found only in south India. Dr George Schaller, the acclaimed American naturalist and field biologist, travelled to the Western Ghats to study the habits and breeding cycle of the Nilgiri Tahr. Describing the Nilgiri Tahr, and other Himalayan sheep and goats, as Mountain Monarchs— he wrote about them in his celebrated work, *Stones of Silence* (1980), in a chapter titled, 'Cloud Goats'.

59. c. Killer Whale

The Killer Whale—averaging about 17 ft. to 19 ft. in size— feeds on warm-blooded and cold-blooded animals. Tigers (8.5 ft. to 10 ft. in size) and Polar Bears (7 ft. to 9 ft. in size) feed on both as well. The Blue Whale—65 ft. to 101 ft. in size—is larger than the Killer Whale, but feeds only on cold-blooded animals.

60. b. Prusten

This type of vocalization is often made by tigers as a greeting, during courtship and when the female communicates with her cubs.

61. b. Echidna

The echidna, also called the spiny anteater, is another one of Australia's unique monotremes. After mating, the female lays a single soft-shelled egg which she keeps in her pouch. After the baby hatches, it feeds on milk and grows in the safety of the mother's pouch.

62. d. Cheetah

63. b. Ganga River Dolphin

64. c. Blackbuck

Salman Khan was accused of killing one Blackbuck and three Chinkara in October 1998 during the shooting of the film, *Hum Saath Saath Hain* (1999). Members of the Bishnoi community lodged a police complaint against actors Saif Ali Khan, Tabu and others. The main accused, however, was Salman Khan, who had also used a gun for which the licence had expired. He was found guilty and was convicted but released on bail. The case is ongoing because Salman Khan has appealed against the verdict and because many witnesses have turned hostile.

65. a. Wild Boar

66. c. Indian Giant Squirrel

67. a. Two

The Slender Loris is found only in south India and Sri Lanka. The Slow Loris is found in Northeast India and parts of Southeast Asia. Both are heavily hunted for the illegal pet-trade and also for traditional medicine. In many Southeast Asian countries, like Thailand, these animals are abused as props for tourist photographs.

Shy by nature and nocturnal, the noise and light cause enormous stress to the animal and damage their sensitive eyes. In many cases, the babies are snatched from their mothers, who are killed, and their teeth are broken to prevent them from biting.

68. d. Camera Traps

State forest departments, the NTCA and the Wildlife Institute of India were involved in the last all-India tiger census. The 2014 report published by the NTCA estimated a tiger population figure of 2226. Data from camera traps and ground surveys was used to estimate abundance and distribution. Camera trapping is an efficient and innovative remote-sensing method in which cameras, equipped with infrared sensors, take pictures whenever they sense movement in the surroundings. Earlier, cameras operated by using film, but today digital cameras, that can take multiple images, are in use. The data is then transferred to a computer for review and analysis.

69. d. *Khairi: The Beloved Tiger*

70. b. Seven

The Gangetic River Dolphin is distributed across Assam, Uttar Pradesh, Madhya Pradesh, Rajasthan, Bihar, Jharkhand and West Bengal.

71. a. Chiru

Although strictly prohibited by law, the Tibetan Antelope, or Chiru, is hunted extensively for its warm wool; its wool is woven into luxury shawls that continue to be in great demand despite a ban. Entire herds, including pregnant females and babies, are gunned down by poachers who travel in high-speed vehicles, chasing the antelopes over great distances. A Chinese railway line runs through the Chiru's feeding and calving grounds in the Tibetan Plateau—this further threatens their survival.

72. c. William Blake

73. b. 350–450

74. b. Leveret

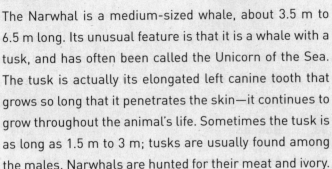

75. d. Narwhal

The Narwhal is a medium-sized whale, about 3.5 m to 6.5 m long. Its unusual feature is that it is a whale with a tusk, and has often been called the Unicorn of the Sea. The tusk is actually its elongated left canine tooth that grows so long that it penetrates the skin—it continues to grow throughout the animal's life. Sometimes the tusk is as long as 1.5 m to 3 m; tusks are usually found among the males. Narwhals are hunted for their meat and ivory.

76. a. Irrawaddy

The Irrawaddy Dolphin is distinct-looking—it is blunt-faced and does not have a beak as most other dolphins do; it also has a very small dorsal fin. In India, it is Critically Endangered and found only in Chilika Lake, Orissa. Habitat degradation, including siltation of the lake, threatens the population.

77. d. Changthang Plateau

78. c. Giraffe

The Okapi was first described by scientists as late as 1901. It's a rich brown in colour and has large ears and a relatively long neck. They also have a long, black tongue with which they pluck buds, leaves and twigs from trees and shrubs. Although the Okapi has white stripes on its hindquarters and legs, as does a zebra, it is most closely related to the Giraffe. The Okapi is found in only one place in the world—in the forests of northeastern Democratic Republic of Congo (DRC).

79. b. Australia

The Dingo is considered a subspecies of the Asian Wolf and was probably introduced in Australia about 4000 years ago. It preys on native animals like kangaroos, and wallabies and rabbits that were introduced. Today, the pure wild Dingo is threatened by interbreeding with domestic dogs.

80. c. Bonobo

81. d. Amur Leopard

82. c. Thirteen

Today, there are only thirteen countries in the world, all in the eastern hemisphere, that have tigers in the wild. These are Bangladesh, Bhutan, Cambodia, China, India, Indonesia, Lao PDR, Malaysia, Myanmar, Nepal, Russia, Thailand and Vietnam.

83. a. South China Tiger

84. c. **Malabar Civet**

85. b. **Warren**

86. c. **Lagomorphs**

87. d. **Hippopotamus**

88. d. **Reindeer**

89. d. **Five fingers and one 'thumb'**

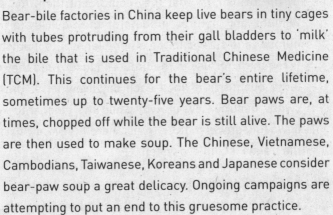

90. a. **Soup**

Bear-bile factories in China keep live bears in tiny cages with tubes protruding from their gall bladders to 'milk' the bile that is used in Traditional Chinese Medicine (TCM). This continues for the bear's entire lifetime, sometimes up to twenty-five years. Bear paws are, at times, chopped off while the bear is still alive. The paws are then used to make soup. The Chinese, Vietnamese, Cambodians, Taiwanese, Koreans and Japanese consider bear-paw soup a great delicacy. Ongoing campaigns are attempting to put an end to this gruesome practice.

91. d. **Chakrashila Wildlife Sanctuary** in Assam

92. b. **Walk with their toes and heels flat on the ground**

93. c. **India**

94. c. **Rafiki**

Rafiki is a character from Walt Disney's animated film, *The Lion King* (1994). Rafiki is a Mandrill and adviser to Mufasa, Simba's father. The male Mandrill has one of the most brightly coloured faces of all species of monkeys—it has white eyelids and a red band running down its nose, with blue protruding bands on either side of it. Its nose is bright red and it has a tufted yellowish beard. Its rear end is also brightly coloured.

95. b. Andaman and Nicobar Islands

Invasive species, like the Chital and the Asiatic Elephant are eating up the forests in the Andaman and Nicobar Islands. Deer were introduced there from the mainland by the British, so that they could hunt them for sport. Without any natural predators, they quickly grew in number and spread to the other islands. Elephants were taken there for use in the timber industry, and they need large quantities of food each day. Now feral, the deer swiftly destroy new growth while the elephants knock down full-grown mature trees, thereby severely harming the fragile island ecosystem.

96. c. Saroj Raj Choudhury

The Tiger Pugmark Method of Census was first used in 1972 to estimate wild tiger numbers in India. This method has been phased out and, in 2014, the tiger population in India was estimated with the help of the modern camera trapping method.

97. c. Madhya Pradesh

Madhya Pradesh is home to six of the country's tiger reserves—namely Kanha, Panna, Bandhavgarh, Pench,

Satpura and Sanjay-Dubri. As per the latest tiger census, Madhya Pradesh has been recorded as having the second-highest tiger population.

98. c. Canines

99. a. Manatee
Both Manatees and Dugongs belong to the order Serenia. However, Manatees are found only in the western hemisphere—in shallow coastal waters, as well as inland—in rivers like the Amazon and Senegal. Dugongs, on the other hand, are found only in the eastern hemisphere and live solely in marine habitats. The Dugong is also called a Sea Cow.

100. d. Armadillo Shell

101.

Sloth Bear	Daroji Wildlife Sanctuary
Nilgiri Tahr	Eravikulam National Park
Swamp Deer	Kanha National Park
Marbled Cat	Balphakram National Park
Gangetic Dolphin	Vikramshila Wildlife Sanctuary

102.

Dr Raghu Chundawat	Snow Leopard
Alan Rabinowitz	Jaguar
Gerald Durrell	Aye-aye
Dr Ullas Karanth	Tiger
George Schaller	Giant Panda

103.

Snow Leopard	Afghanistan
Jaguar	Mexico
Tiger	Bangladesh
Giraffe	Tanzania
Lion	Ethiopia

104.

Joey	Kangaroo
Pup	Bat
Foal	Wild Ass
Cria	Llama
Calf	Dugong

105.

Meerkat	Timon, *The Lion King*
Reindeer	Sven, *Frozen*
Skunk	Flower, *Bambi*
Ring-tailed Lemur	King Julian, *Madagascar*
Indian Wolf	Akela, *The Jungle Book*

106.

Barasingha	Madhya Pradesh
Indian Elephant	Kerala
Blackbuck	Andhra Pradesh
Fishing Cat	West Bengal
Clouded Leopard	Meghalaya

107. Orange-red

The Blue Whale, the world's largest animal, feeds mainly on tons of tiny krill. It secretes huge amounts of faeces which are bright orange-red—similar in colour to krill. It can be spotted from far away when it floats on the water surface, and is an indication that there is a Blue Whale in the area. Whale faeces contribute greatly to the health of the marine ecosystem.

108. Arctic Ocean

109. Hoolock Gibbon

The endangered Hoolock Gibbon is slender and graceful. A bonded pair of gibbons will sing a haunting duet from dawn till noon to protect their territory from other gibbons. Human activities have decimated gibbon populations by about 90 per cent.

110. Four

The lion, tiger, leopard and Snow Leopard.

111. Sea Otter

112. India

Besides its use in cooking, palm oil is used in manufacturing soap, shampoo, detergent, candles and other day-to-day products. Destruction of natural habitats for palm oil cultivation also threatens tigers, rhinos and elephants with extinction. Production and use of certified sustainable palm oil could reduce the damage.

113. From the shape of its dorsal fin

The male's dorsal fin is large and straight, while the female's is curved or sickle-shaped.

114. 29 July

115. Aye-aye

The endangered Aye-aye is a strange-looking nocturnal primate that is found only in Madagascar. It lives in trees and is omnivorous—it feeds on fruit, seeds and insects. It has a special adaptation—an elongated middle finger that it uses to tap tree branches to locate grubs. It uses its rodent-like teeth to chew a hole into the branch and, with its elongated finger, pulls the grub out.

116. For manufacturing drums

117. Pangolin

The Pangolin is the only known mammal with scales.

118. Indira Gandhi

Project Tiger was launched soon after this, in 1973.

119. Golden Jackal or Common Jackal

120. Rajwada, Madhya Pradesh

121. Leopard

122. Maldharis in Gujarat

123. Toilet Claw or Grooming Claw

124. Mob or Clan or Gang

125. Gangetic River Dolphin

126. About 6 ft.

127. Mouse Deer

The Indian Chevrotain or Mouse Deer is a tiny, shy, secretive and mainly nocturnal animal. Once widely distributed, it is now found mostly in south India.

128. Dromedary

129. Keratin

The Scaly Anteater, also called the pangolin, is a major part of the illegal wildlife trade and is hunted for its scales and meat. In 2013, around 10,000 kg of pangolin meat was seized from a Chinese boat. All pangolin species are Critically Endangered.

130. Indian 10-rupee Banknote

131. Ambergris

Ambergris is secreted in the whale's intestine, and is discharged in its faeces. When it's fresh, it is soft, dark in colour and has an unpleasant odour. It hardens and turns lighter over time, and develops a sweetish smell. It can be found floating in the ocean or washed up on the beach. Beaks of the Giant Squid—the favourite prey of Sperm Whales—have been found in ambergris. Perfumers making high-quality perfumes buy ambergris only from trusted brokers. In 2013, a dog walker on a UK beach was offered around US $50,000 for a lump of ambergris that his dog had found.

132. Antelope

This medium-sized antelope species is also known as the Vaal Rhebok. It prefers rugged terrain, and is found only in a small region of the plateau and mountain grasslands of Southern Africa. In the wild, it lives for about eight to ten years.

133. Brazil

134. Spotted Deer or Chital

The two species have a symbiotic relationship.

135. Beavers

136. Underground Burrows

137. Fruit Bats

138. Stallion

139. Billy Arjan Singh

In 1981, Billy Arjan Singh, a hunter-turned-conservationist, wrote a book about his life with the tiger cub titled *Tara: A Tigress*.

140. By their colour

Adult females are light brown or buff, whereas the adult males are dark brown or blackish-brown.

141. Woolly Mammoth

142. Indian Wild Dog or Dhole

143. Dachigam National Park

144. Blue Whale

145. Marco Polo

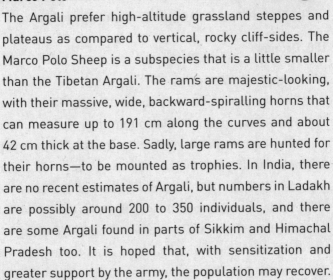

The Argali prefer high-altitude grassland steppes and plateaus as compared to vertical, rocky cliff-sides. The Marco Polo Sheep is a subspecies that is a little smaller than the Tibetan Argali. The rams are majestic-looking, with their massive, wide, backward-spiralling horns that can measure up to 191 cm along the curves and about 42 cm thick at the base. Sadly, large rams are hunted for their horns—to be mounted as trophies. In India, there are no recent estimates of Argali, but numbers in Ladakh are possibly around 200 to 350 individuals, and there are some Argali found in parts of Sikkim and Himachal Pradesh too. It is hoped that, with sensitization and greater support by the army, the population may recover.

146. It is the only mammal in the world with four horns

147. Northeast India

148. Milk

The Killer Whale is a toothed whale, an apex predator, and the largest of all dolphin species. They live in family groups or pods; the males usually mate with females from a different pod. The females give birth to one calf each, and continue to feed it milk—high in fat—for the first year of its life—sometimes for even as long as two years. Killer Whales have no natural predators but are hunted by humans for meat and oil, and held in captivity for amusement at sea parks.

149. Female Asiatic Elephants have no tusks, while both male and female African Elephants have tusks

150. Drones

151. Humpback Whale

The Humpback Whale (around 11 m to 18 m in size) is a species of baleen whales that migrates thousands of kilometres from the poles to the tropics. They are popular subjects for most whale-watching trips and are easily identified by their huge size, their throat-pleats—that enable them to open their mouths very wide—and their very long flippers. The male Humpback Whale produces long and unique vocalizations, often during the mating season. Research shows that whales from a particular area sing similar songs, while those from another region have a different song.

152. Fat reserves stored in their body

153. Vibrissae

The Walrus forages for clams and other invertebrates living on the seabed. It uses its tusks to stir up the sand, and senses prey movement with its thick, bristly whiskers, called vibrissae. The vibrissae, connected to muscles, are sensitive tactile organs.

154. Bactrian

155. Gorillas

Coltan is the short form of the ore known as columbite–tantalite. It is dull black in colour, and is used in the production of many electronic devices, including mobile phones. Mining for coltan has resulted in the pollution of water sources as well as habitat destruction. Some miners hunt the adult gorillas for meat, and steal the infants for illegal trade.

156. Person of the Forest

157. Orca

158. Zimbabwe

After the huge uproar over the shooting of Cecil, many reputed and responsible airlines announced that they would no longer carry any wildlife trophies on their flights.

159. Vietnam

Pangolins are found in Africa and Asia. Vietnam is home to two species of the pangolin, both of which are protected by law. However, most of the Vietnamese population, with their growing prosperity, are buyers and consumers of protected wildlife and its derivatives, including of pangolins. While restaurants serve pangolin meat as a speciality, bars serve wine with pangolins soaked in it. The blood is consumed by people to keep warm and to boost their health, and the scales are used in traditional medicine.

160. Ebola

Ebola is a virus that spreads through the blood and other body fluids of humans and animals. The disease was first identified in an outbreak in a village near the River Ebola in Zaire, from which it gets its name. Fruit bats are thought to be carriers, and human consumption of wild animals, like monkeys and apes, spreads the disease. According to some conservationists and scientists, Ebola has wiped out as much as one-third of the gorilla and chimpanzee populations.

BIRDS

Widely accepted by paleontologists as an early bird, the pigeon-sized Archaeopteryx lived in the Jurassic Period. Well-preserved fossils of this dinosaur-like animal, with flight feathers similar to those of modern birds, were found in the second half of the 19th century.

Although the main structure of birds has changed little since those ancient times—modern birds are varied in form, colour and vocalization. Belonging to the class Aves, these warm-blooded, feathered animals have beaks, no teeth and lay hard-shelled eggs.

Popular as religious and cultural icons, wild birds have always fascinated humans with their flight, song and beauty. Valued as pollinators, birds are also an important source of food and livelihood. Air travel, inspired by birds, can be considered a feather in the cap of our avian friends! The word aviation itself is a derivative of 'avis', the Latin word for 'bird'.

In return for their limitless gifts, however, we cull, cage, hunt and modify them to suit our needs.

Questions

1 The spotting of which bird is said to signal the arrival of the monsoon in India?

a. Pied Cuckoo

b. Indian Peafowl

c. Asian Koel

d. Rosy Pelican

2 Which was the group of birds on the Galapagos Islands that Charles Darwin studied to establish his theory of evolution of species?

a. Starlings

b. Eagles

c. Finches

d. Ducks

3 Which flightless bird, from the Edinburgh Zoo, was given the prestigious honour of a knighthood in 2008, approved by King Harald V of Norway?

a. Kiwi

b. Ostrich

c. Penguin

d. Dodo

4 This bird, with the longest wingspan—of about 3.5 m—features in *The Rime of the Ancient Mariner* (1798) by poet Samuel Taylor Coleridge. To which of these birds does Coleridge refer?

a. Wandering Albatross

b. Bearded Vulture

c. Andean Condor

d. Ostrich

5 Hunted for the illegal pet-trade, which Brazilian parrot species has not been seen in the wild since the year 2000?

a. Spix's Macaw
b. Kakapo
c. Echo Parakeet
d. Orange-bellied Parrot

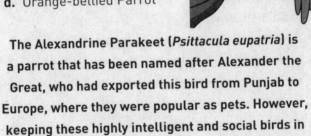

The Alexandrine Parakeet (*Psittacula eupatria*) is a parrot that has been named after Alexander the Great, who had exported this bird from Punjab to Europe, where they were popular as pets. However, keeping these highly intelligent and social birds in cages is like keeping an ape or a human in solitary confinement!

6 Which of these birds lays the largest egg relative to its size?

a. Kiwi
b. Ostrich
c. Bald Eagle
d. Pigeon

7 Which of these Indian birds makes its nest and lays its eggs in the pagoda-like nest of the arboreal Acrobat Ant?

a. Magpie Robin
b. Drongo
c. Asian Cuckoo
d. Rufous Woodpecker

Cameras installed in the nests of endangered
vultures have shown chicks dying of hunger. The
Maharashtra forest department plans to open
'vulture restaurants' to provide food to the vultures
near nesting areas.

8 In the 1990s, 98 per cent of the vulture population in
India died. Why?
a. They were hunted for eating beef
b. Roadkills—they got run over while feeding
c. They ate dead cattle that had been treated with an
anti-inflammatory drug
d. Due to loss of habitat

The woodpecker is considered to be sacred to
Mars, the Roman god of war. Woodpeckers have
strong, chisel-like beaks that they use to drill
into trees in order to extract grubs with their
long, sticky tongues.

9 Owners of which type of birds run an increased risk
of Psittacosis, a zoonotic infectious disease—one that
can pass between humans and animals?
a. Parakeets   b. Budgerigars
c. Macaws   d. All of these

10 Poisoning by which pesticide contributed to the near-
extinction of the Bald Eagle, America's national bird?

The pesticide was finally banned in the US in the 1970s.

a. Diclofenac
b. Quinine
c. DDT
d. DEET

11 While most birds have three or four toes, which species has only two toes on each foot?

a. Parrot
b. Crow
c. Ostrich
d. Kite

12 In the 19th century, the Passenger Pigeon was one of the most numerous birds in the world, with a population of around five billion. Subjected to habitat loss, hunting and disease—how many of these remain today?

a. About 10 billion
b. About 10 million
c. About 10,000
d. 0

Did you know that the ostrich is killed for its meat, skin and feathers? While its meat is consumed, its skin is used to produce high-quality leather and its feathers are used in the fashion industry.

13 The colour of the bald head and neck of the Critically Endangered Red-headed Vulture ranges from deep red to red-orange. By which other name is this bird commonly known?

a. Indian King Vulture   b. Indian Black Vulture

c. Pondicherry Vulture   d. All of these

14 Which of these birds is not a raptor?

a. Crow   b. Owl

c. Vulture   d. Eagle

15 Many perching birds use insects to help them get rid of lice from their feathers. Which insects do they use?

a. Flies   b. Bees

c. Cockroaches   d. Ants

During the kite-flying season in Delhi, as many as a hundred birds a day may get entangled and injured— or even killed—by the dangerously sharp China-made 'manjha' or string, used for kite-flying. A bird-friendly alternative is urgently needed. Can you think of any?

16 Adult flamingoes are easily recognizable because they are large and pink in colour; what colour is the chick?

a. Pink   b. Red

c. Brown   d. Grey

17 Exactly how did DDT adversely affect the Bald Eagle in the US, eventually threatening it with extinction? It caused _____.

a. Kidney Failure
b. Heart Attack
c. Weak Eggshells
d. Food Shortage

18 Dovecoting is a method of controlling the bird population. In this strategy, bird houses—for nesting—are placed in suitable locations and, then, the laid eggs are replaced with artificial eggs. For which bird has this been used?

a. Pigeons
b. Vultures
c. Jungle Fowl
d. Parakeets

'Sing a song of sixpence,
A pocket full of rye.
Four and twenty blackbirds,
Baked in a pie.
When the pie was opened,
The birds began to sing;
Wasn't that a dainty dish,
To set before the king?'

This famous English rhyme talks about actual dishes which were fashionable in the 18th century, which were meant to be eaten as much as they were meant

to entertain. One such dish was a pie cooked with live
birds which, when cut, would have the birds fly out!
Whether the birds survived or not is unclear.

19 Which naturalist first named and described the
Black-necked Crane in 1876, the last of the fifteen
crane species to be discovered?
a. Carl Linnaeus
b. Nikolay Przewalski
c. Dr Salim Ali
d. A.O. Hume

20 What is a male swan called?
a. Cock
b. Cob
c. Gander
d. Drake

21 Which of these bird groups has adopted brood
parasitism as a survival mechanism?
a. Cowbirds
b. Cuckoos
c. African Finches
d. All of these

22 Which of these penguins belongs to the group of
crested penguins and displays prominent yellow
feathers on both sides of its head?
a. Royal Penguin
b. Rockhopper Penguin
c. Macaroni Penguin
d. All of these

23 Which small raptor, with one of the longest migratory routes in the world, has been slaughtered in thousands in Northeast India?

a. Peregrine Falcon   b. Amur Falcon

c. Shikra   d. Merlin

24 A tombstone was erected in the Bronx Zoo for this endemic Indian species, presumed extinct in 1900. Fortunately, it was rediscovered in 1986. Which Critically Endangered bird is this?

a. Great Indian Bustard   b. Narcondam Hornbill

c. Indian Vulture   d. Jerdon's Courser

25 Who is famously known as the Birdman of India?

a. Dr Asad Rehmani

b. Dr Salim Ali

c. Jim Corbett

d. Kartick Satyanarayan

Though many species of the parrot family are kept as pets in India, most people do not realize that what they are doing is illegal and punishable by law.

26 Both the world's tallest and the smallest crane species can be spotted in India. The tallest is the Sarus; which is the smallest?

a. Common Crane   b. Siberian Crane

c. Demoiselle Crane   d. Black-necked Crane

27 Some birds, such as flamingoes and doves, feed a protein secretion from their oesophagus to their offspring. What is this known as?

a. Egg Yolk

b. Albumin

c. Insect Mash

d. Crop Milk

28 In which of these places would you find penguins?

a. The Arctic

b. The Antarctic

c. Iceland

d. All of these

29 Which is the only flightless parrot species in the world?

a. Kea

b. Rock Conure

c. Kakapo

d. Vernal Hanging Parrot

Aristophanes, the Greek playwright, wrote a prize-winning comic play called, *The Birds*. In this play, the king, Tereus, is changed into—would you believe it—a hoopoe! The play, performed at the City Dionysia festival in Athens, in 414 BC, won the second prize.

30 Which is the safe alternative to diclofenac, the anti-inflammatory drug that caused a drastic decline in India's vulture population?

a. Ketoprofen

b. Naproxen

c. Bromfenac

d. Meloxicam

31 Endemic to the Indian subcontinent, this bird is on the brink of extinction; there are only around

150 of this species left in India. Which bird is this?

a. Pink-headed Duck
b. Great Indian Bustard
c. Himalayan Monal
d. Lammergeier

According to sailors, seeing a swallow while out at sea is a lucky sign. This is probably because swallows are land birds and are usually seen close to the shore, so seeing one from the ship meant that the sailors were nearing land.

32 What kind of nest is usually made by kingfishers?
a. Floating Nest
b. Tunnel Nest
c. Pendant Nest
d. All of these

33 Discovered in 2006, in Arunachal Pradesh this new species is on IUCN's Red List as Critically Endangered. Which bird is this?
a. Black-necked Crane
b. Mascarene Petrel
c. Bugun Liocichla
d. Orange Bullfinch

34 In which Indian state is the Choolanur Peacock Sanctuary, created specifically for the protection of peafowl, located?
a. Kerala
b. Andhra Pradesh
c. Orissa
d. Karnataka

35 Which bird was the mascot for the 35th National Games of India, held in Kerala in February 2015?

a. Greater Flamingo

b. Greater Adjutant Stork

c. Great Indian Bustard

d. Great Indian Hornbill

36 After years of feeding and protection by the villagers, Demoiselle Cranes have made a certain Indian village famous for a large winter population. Which village is this?

a. Etawah

b. Khichan

c. Bharatpur

d. Pangti

37 Which of these is not a group of birds, but a group of weasel-like mammals?

a. Accipiters

b. Shrikes

c. Frogmouths

d. Martens

Sirocco, a Kakapo, is the government-appointed 'Official Spokesbird for Conservation' of New Zealand. The Kakapo is the world's heaviest parrot species, and weighs about 2000 g to 4000 g— around the weight of a small dog!

38 Many cranes are migratory. Which of these is the only non-migratory, resident species of India?

a. Siberian Crane **b.** Demoiselle Crane

c. Black-necked Crane **d.** Sarus Crane

39 Adult flamingoes turn a wonderful shade of pink as they grow. What gives the bird its pink colour?

a. Exposure to the sun **b.** The food it eats

c. Industrial pollution **d.** All of these

40 Hudhud, the name given to the massive cyclone that hit the eastern coast of India in October 2014, is also the local name of a bird. Which one?

a. Harrier

b. Hoopoe

c. Nightjar

d. Bulbul

Did you know that, in 2015, the robin won an important election in Britain? Thousands of people voted for this little songster to be their national bird. The robin emerged as the winner against ten other birds, including bigger ones like the Barn Owl, the Red Kite, the Mute Swan and others.

41 Their traditional burials have become almost impossible due to the decline in the vulture

population. Which religious community in
India has been particularly affected by the
absence of vultures?

a. Hindu

b. Muslim

c. Jain

d. Parsi

42 Which is the only Indian bird that feeds itself by using
its feet to bring food up to its mouth?

a. Parakeet

b. Kingfisher

c. Vulture

d. Bustard

43 The Lammergeier, which has been observed carrying
bones high up in the air and dropping them on rocks
below, is also known as the _____.

a. Slender-billed Vulture

b. White-rumped Vulture

c. Bearded Vulture

d. Red-headed Vulture

Prayas, an NGO in Gujarat, has launched a mobile
app called the Bird Tap in Surat to help thirsty birds
get a drink of water. Users can get earthen water-
pots from registered centres to keep in gardens and
homes, for birds to drink from. Isn't that a great idea?

44 Many birds are sexually dimorphic i.e., the males and females look distinctly different. Which of these birds is not sexually dimorphic?

a. Peafowl

b. Koel

c. Sparrow

d. Penguin

45 Which of these beautiful birds is the state bird of at least five Indian states?

a. Indian Roller

b. Asian Paradise Flycatcher

c. Great Hornbill

d. Himalayan Monal

46 Commercially valuable as a fertilizer, what is the excreta of seabirds called?

a. Spraint

b. Tath

c. Ambergris

d. Guano

47 The Little Penguin is the smallest and weighs around 1 kg. At approximately 40 kg, which is the largest penguin?

a. King Penguin

b. Emperor Penguin

c. Adélie Penguin

d. Gentoo Penguin

48 Match the bird with its preferred food:

Kingfisher	Fruit
Sunbird	Dead Animals
Indian Roller	Fish
Vulture	Insects
Parakeet	Nectar

The Blue-footed Booby (*Sula nebouxii*), a sea bird, is easily recognized by its large webbed feet, which are bright blue in colour. Female birds prefer males with the brightest coloured feet, since this shows that he is healthy, strong and will make a good father.

49 Match the bird with their type of nest:

Swiftlet	Pendant Nest
Bulbul	Mound Nest
Baya	Saliva and Mud Nest
Flamingo	Floating Nest
Jacana	Cup Nest

50 This Ramsar Site is the largest coastal lagoon in India. It is the wintering ground for a large number of migratory birds. Which state is the lagoon in?

51 The Chukar or Chakor is a beautiful ground-nesting bird from the pheasant family, with attractive black-and-white markings. It has a distinctive black band that extends from its head and encircles its throat like a necklace. Which countries have adopted it as their national bird?

Cockfighting, like bullfighting, is a cruel, bloody sport and is banned in India. However, it still takes place in many parts of the country, including Andhra Pradesh and Tamil Nadu. In the sport, a pair of gamecocks are made to fight each other until one is critically injured or dead.

52 Of which Indian state is the Great Indian Bustard— now rarer than a tiger and extinct in 90 per cent of its earlier geographical range—the state bird?

53 Which Indian forest bird is known for the human quality of its calls, that can be heard mainly at dawn? It is popularly nicknamed as the Whistling Schoolboy.

54 Of the fifteen species of cranes found worldwide, how many are now seen in India?

The adult Sarus Crane is an elegant grey, with a naked red head that looks like it has been dipped in blood! A bonded pair of Sarus Cranes usually raise one chick, who is brown in colour.

55 Which owl species nests and roosts underground in a burrow?

56 The lower half of this bird's bill can hold more food than its stomach can. Which bird is this?

57 Birds sit on their eggs and keep them warm to hatch them. What is this activity called?

58 Which rare hornbill, found only on one island in India, is threatened by habitat destruction due to a radar-station project? The project was halted in 2012 but was given approval in 2014.

59 This tall bird, found in India, wades in water with its beak held upside down and filters out brine shrimp with it. Which bird feeds in this unique way?

A famous 17th-century Mughal artist in Emperor Jahangir's court, Ustad Mansur, is said to have painted one of the few existing images of the Dodo from a live specimen. Emperor Jahangir was very interested in wildlife and had an extensive menagerie in Surat.

60 What did Rudyard Kipling name the Tailorbird that featured in his popular story, 'Rikki-Tilkki-Tavi'?

61 What kind of diet does the Malabar Whistling Thrush, a well-known songster of the Indian forests, have?

62 What is the decorative horn-like growth on a hornbill's beak called?

63 What is the main cause that threatens the wild Red Jungle Fowl with extinction?

Have you read the book *Salim Ali for Schools* by Zai Whitaker?

64 In September 2015, a new scientific study reported a particular substance found in the guts of around 90 per cent of seabirds. What was it?

65 A large company is building a hydropower dam in the Tawang Valley of Arunachal Pradesh. Which large, rare bird species will be affected by this?

66 There are only three existing species of this large bird from the pheasant family—two are found in Asia and one is found in the Congo Basin in Africa. Which bird is this?

67 Which wild bird is the ancestor of the domestic chicken, on which the multibillion-dollar poultry industry is based?

200

68 Owls cannot chew and often swallow their prey whole—bones, teeth, fur, feathers and all. In what form do they later cough up the waste?

Two places in India where you can see the Black-necked Crane are Ladakh in Jammu, and Kashmir and Zimithang in Arunachal Pradesh.

69 Now extinct, Martha was the last living individual of this once-numerous North American bird. It is said that a flock of these birds took around three days to pass overhead. To which species did Martha belong?

Do you know the connection between the decrease of the vulture population and the increase in deaths by rabies in India? This is because the number of stray dogs—especially in villages—has increased due to more food i.e., dead cattle being available to them now, since there are far fewer scavenging birds around. More dogs lead to more dog bites, and more dog bites lead to more cases of rabies.

70 Whose autobiography is the book, *The Fall of a Sparrow*?

Answers

1. **a. Pied Cuckoo**
    The Pied Cuckoo or the Jacobin Cuckoo is a crested black-and-white bird that is a summer visitor to most parts of India. Its arrival is said to coincide with the outbreak of the monsoon season. Like many other cuckoos, this bird is a brood parasite; relying on a host to raise its young, it does not make its own nest, but lays its eggs in the nest of another bird, who works hard catching insects to feed the cuckoo-chick after it hatches.

2. **c. Finches**
    Darwin's Finches are a group of birds with distinctly different types of beaks that are clearly adapted to the type of food that they eat. Charles Darwin studied the specialized beaks and related feeding habits of the birds, and his findings influenced his theory of evolution based on natural selection.

3. **c. Penguin**

A King Penguin, named Nils Olav, was awarded knighthood by the Norwegian Royal Guard at a ceremony held at the Edinburgh Zoo in 2008. He is the mascot and honorary member of the Norwegian battalion. The King Penguin is a large, sleek, black-and-white bird with striking golden-orange markings on its head and upper chest. Its chicks are brown and fuzzy, and do not resemble the adult birds until they moult.

4. **a. Wandering Albatross**

The Wandering Albatross is a huge seabird which is found flying over oceans, mainly in the southern hemisphere. Almost completely white as adults, the juvenile birds have brownish bodies with white faces. A pair of Wandering Albatrosses is said to mate for life and breeds once in two years. They are threatened by longline fishing, which is the main cause of the rapid decline in this species's population.

5. **a. Spix's Macaw**

Spix's Macaw, a beautiful medium-sized parrot whose feathers are varying shades of blue, is one of the rarest birds. It was found only in a small forest-patch in northeast Brazil, but even the single bird that was living there has not been spotted since 2000. It has been classified as Critically Endangered (Possibly Extinct in the Wild). Its habitat is being gradually destroyed, and most of the birds have been hunted for the pet trade. Organizations, like the Association for the Conservation of Threatened Parrots (ACTP), are working to reintroduce Spix Macaws, bred in captivity, back into the wild.

6. a. **Kiwi**

7. d. **Rufous Woodpecker**

8. c. **They ate dead cattle that had been treated with an anti-inflammatory drug**

The chemicals in the drug, diclofenac, commonly used by vets to treat many minor medical problems in cows, buffaloes and other livestock, causes kidney failure and death in the vultures that consume the carcasses of these treated animals. Even tiny amounts of the drug are fatal to vultures. This has led to the death of almost all the vultures in India. Because of this, dead bodies of animals lying in fields or roads continue to rot, causing pollution and disease. Additionally, infection-causing animals like flies, rats and feral dogs have also increased in number. The loss of vultures in India has resulted in sanitation and medical costs worth billions of rupees.

9. d. **All of these**

All birds of the parrot family, also called psittacine birds, are carriers of the bacterium that causes Psittacosis, and can infect their handlers with this disease. This zoonotic disease is also known as parrot fever.

10. c. DDT (dichlorodiphenyltrichloroethane)

The Bald Eagle is not really bald, but has white feathers on its head and dark brown feathers on its body. It is a powerful bird with a wingspan of 6 to 8 ft. It was adopted as the national symbol of America in the 18th century when it was numerous. After it was hunted almost to extinction, the US Government passed the Bald Eagle Protection Act in 1940. However, excessive use of the pesticide, DDT, in the 1940s and 50s, and its subsequent effects on the food chain—reported by Rachel Carson in her 1962 book, *Silent Spring*—resulted in reproductive problems for many birds, especially the Bald Eagle. Finally, in 1972, DDT was banned in the United States and, since then, Bald Eagle numbers have improved. Unfortunately, in India—one of the few countries that still make DDT—the government is still debating on whether or not to ban its use.

11. c. Ostrich

12. d. 0

13. d. All of these

14. a. Crow

Raptors are birds of prey. Usually medium to large in size, they hunt and feed on other animals. Raptors have very good eyesight, sharp curved beaks and strong talons with which they grasp their prey. Crows are mainly scavenging birds.

15. d. Ants

16. d. Grey

17. c. Weak Eggshells
Contamination of the Bald Eagle's food, due to DDT, caused the birds to lay eggs with weak shells which broke during incubation itself. With fewer chicks hatching, Bald Eagle numbers fell very low, and this majestic bird reached the brink of extinction in the 1970s.

18. a. Pigeons

19. b. Nikolay Przewalski
The Black-necked Crane, also called the Tibetan Crane, is the only alpine crane in the world and is native to China, Bhutan and India. Unique among cranes, this species inhabits high-altitude remote areas of the Tibetan Plateau and Himalayas. Breeding in wetland areas, it lays up to two eggs in a nest made of mud, grass and aquatic plants. Both the male and female share incubation duty, and the male aggressively defends the chicks.

20. b. Cob

21. d. All of these
Usually brood parasites lay only one egg in a host bird's nest. In some cases, the hosts recognize and remove the egg, but some birds incubate and feed the parasite

chick even though it is much larger than its own chicks, sometimes growing even larger than the host parent.

22. d. All of these

23. b. Amur Falcon

24. d. Jerdon's Courser

The Critically Endangered Jerdon's Courser is a small sand-coloured, nocturnal bird that nests on the ground. It is found only in south India, and was first described in 1848 by ornithologist Thomas Jerdon, after whom it is named. Since 1900, there had been no recorded sightings, and people thought that the bird was extinct. The Bronx Zoo in New York even erected a tombstone in its memory. However, in 1986, much to the delight of bird-watchers all over the world, scientists from the Bombay Natural History Society (BNHS) sighted it once again. Destruction of its scrub forest habitat—for agricultural use—continue to threaten this bird.

25. b. Dr Salim Ali

Well-known for his minute observations and detailed notes on the birds that he'd studied, the great ornithologist, Dr Salim Ali, did not have a formal university degree early in his career. He later got his scientific training by working with a famous professor, Dr Erwin Stresemann, at Berlin University. Because of his detailed knowledge about the birds of India, Bombay University awarded him an honorary doctorate. Dr Ali was so passionate about birds and their conservation, that, in 1976, at eighty years of age, he led a scientific expedition to Ladakh to study the habitat and survey the numbers of the rare Black-necked Crane. This excursion was the first of its kind in fifty years.

26. c. Demoiselle Crane

27. d. Crop Milk
Some kinds of birds produce a milk-like substance, which is fed to their chicks in the first few days of their growth. It contains antioxidants and immunity-building proteins just as human milk does.

28. b. The Antarctic

29. c. Kakapo
The Kakapo is a large, nocturnal species of parrot, which cannot fly. It is found only in New Zealand and since it had no natural predators, it lost the ability to fly and it nests on the ground. However, European settlers found the birds easy prey, since they had no aerial escape. The settlers, and the mammals that they'd introduced, took to eating the adult birds, their chicks and eggs. At one time, there were no Kakapos left in the wild but, then, some birds were discovered in 1977, on Stewart Island, New Zealand. There may be as few as about 125 Kakapos left.

30. d. Meloxicam

31. b. Great Indian Bustard

32. b. Tunnel Nest

33. c. Bugun Liocichla
First spotted in 1995 in the Eaglenest Wildlife Sanctuary, this rare, small bird was first described by Ramana Athreya in 2006. About the size of a babbler, it is olive-green in colour with a black cap, and bright red, yellow and white patches on the wings. This was said to be one of the most exciting bird discoveries in India in the last fifty years and Dr Athreya has won several awards for his work.

34. a. Kerala

35. d. Great Indian Hornbill

36. b. Khichan
For most of the year, Khichan, near Jodhpur in Rajasthan, is a quiet sleepy village. However, due to the generosity and tolerance of the villagers, this place becomes a haven for thousands of migrating Demoiselle Cranes each winter. About fifty years ago, just a few cranes used to visit and were fed grain by the villagers. Gradually, the number of visitors have increased and, today, thousands of cranes can be seen in Khichan sometimes.

37. d. Martens
Martins are perching birds that resemble the swallow and can feed while flying; Martens are small, furry, carnivorous mammals, related to weasels and otters.

38. d. Sarus Crane

All cranes call and dance as part of their courtship ritual; the performance of a bonded pair of Sarus Cranes is touching to watch. It includes both birds bowing to each other, prancing and leaping to haunting, synchronized calls. It is said that if one of the pair is killed, the other pines away and dies.

39. b. The food it eats

When flamingoes hatch, they are grey in colour but after feeding on a special diet of brine shrimp and algae, they turn a beautiful shade of pink as adults. This is because their natural diet in the wild is rich in a pigment called carotenoid. In some zoos, flamingoes need to be given synthetic carotenoids if they start losing their bright plumage. Some fruits and vegetables, such as mangoes, sweet potatoes and carrots—orange or red in colour— are also rich in carotenoids.

40. b. Hoopoe

41. d. Parsi

Parsis or Zoroastrians—followers of Zarathustra— believe that earth and fire are both sacred, and therefore do not burn or bury their dead. Instead, they prefer to dispose of the dead by placing their bodies in structures known as the Towers of Silence. Here, scavenging birds— mainly vultures—quickly consume the corpses. This practice is called 'Dokhmenashini'. However, because of the drastic drop in the vulture population of India, the disposal of their dead has become problematic for the Parsi community. Additionally, although diclofenac is banned for veterinary use, it is still available for human use, and therefore vultures are not safe from its effects.

42. a. **Parakeet**

43. c. **Bearded Vulture**

44. d. **Penguin**

The males and females of many animals, particularly birds, look very different from each other in colour, size, shape and structure. In most penguins, the males and females look similar. The best example of dimorphism is seen among peafowl; while the peacock is larger, brightly coloured and very attractive, the peahen is smaller and drab-looking.

45. a. **Indian Roller**

46. d. **Guano**

47. b. **Emperor Penguin**

48.

Kingfisher	Fish
Sunbird	Nectar
Indian Roller	Insects
Vulture	Dead Animals
Parakeet	Fruit

49.

Baya	Pendant Nest
Flamingo	Mound Nest
Swiftlet	Saliva and Mud Nest
Jacana	Floating Nest
Bulbul	Cup Nest

50. Orissa, Chilika lake

Chilika Lake in Orissa is an 'Important Bird Area' (IBA) and—as all IBAs do—enjoys international recognition. These sites are identified by BirdLife International—a partnership of organizations from around the world which work together for the conservation of birds. The Chilika Lake has recorded over 200 species of migratory and resident birds and, besides this, Orissa hosts around six other IBAs.

51. Pakistan and Iraq

The omnivorous Chakor partridge is found in India, Pakistan, Afghanistan and other parts of Asia and Europe. It has been introduced into the United States where it is popular with hunters. In Indian mythology, the bird is said to thirst for the moon, and is a symbol of unrequited love. In parts of Asia, the cock is also used as a fighting bird, with people placing bets on which bird will win.

52. Rajasthan

53. Malabar Whistling Thrush
The Malabar Whistling Thrush lives in forested areas near streams, and makes a cup-shaped ground-nest—of roots, moss and grass—reinforced with mud.

54. Four
The Sarus Crane, Demoiselle Crane, Common Crane and Black-necked Crane are seen in India. The fifth species that could be seen earlier—the Siberian Crane—would winter at Bharatpur, but a pair was last spotted there in 2002. It is now locally extinct due to the disturbance of its migratory route, attributed to the Afghan War.

55. Burrowing Owl

56. Pelican

57. Incubation

58. Narcondam Hornbill

59. Flamingo

60. Darzee
The word stands for 'tailor' in Hindi and Urdu.

61. Omnivorous

62. Casque

63. Cross-breeding or hybridization with domestic chickens

64. Plastics

Senior researchers have published a study on the contents that were found in seabirds' stomachs. Seabirds, like albatrosses and shearwaters, mistake bits of plastic for fish and fish eggs, and eat them. Plastic items, like cigarette lighters, bottle caps and small toys, have been found in their stomachs. Marine turtles have also been found to consume plastic bags. Improving human waste management and reducing our use of plastic are extremely important to avoid such harmful intake by unsuspecting creatures.

65. Black-necked Crane

The dam will divert the Nyamjang Chhu River and destroy the habitat of several endangered species, including this particular wintering site of the rare Black-necked Crane.

66. Peafowl

The three species of existing peafowl are the Indian Peafowl, the Green Peafowl and the Congo Peafowl. The Indian Peafowl is one of the best-known birds in the world, and features in Indian and Greek mythology. However—discovered only in the 1930s—comparatively little was known about the Congo Peafowl, a shy and elusive bird. The male has vibrant metallic-blue chest and tail feathers, but is not as beautiful as the Indian species. It has a crest of distinctive white bristles on the top of its head and some dark feathers behind. The white peafowl, a mutation of the Indian Peafowl, is sometimes seen in captivity but rarely found in the wild.

67. Red Junglefowl

68. Pellets

Owls—birds of prey—are mostly nocturnal. They have sharp eyesight, and can fly swiftly and silently. Good hunters, they eat small animals like insects, rats and lizards. The parts that they cannot digest like hair, bones, teeth and feathers are compressed in the owl's digestive system and are coughed up in the form of pellets. Scientists studying these birds collect and analyse the pellets to inspect what they have been eating.

69. Passenger Pigeon

The Passenger Pigeon—a species of wild pigeons—once found in large numbers in the deciduous forests of North America, is now extinct. Although very fast-flying, they were defenceless against the guns of European settlers, who hunted them in huge numbers and cut down trees which provided them with fruit. The last wild bird was shot in the 1900s. There were a few pigeons left in captivity, but Martha—the last of these—died in the Cincinnati Zoo in 1914.

70. Dr Salim Ali

As a young boy, Dr Salim Ali was not very interested in schoolwork—he joked that he took up bird watching just to avoid doing his homework! Although he did not have a formal university degree at the start of his career— whenever he talked to students, he always encouraged them to get 'that piece of paper' which he discovered was actually very important when he was applying for a job that he wanted.

POTPOURRI

Now here's the best for the last—a little of this, a little of that, and a little of us thrown in! Here's the bit about people, places, policy, folklore and all sorts of assorted wild facts.

Enjoy while you wait for more!

Questions

1 Roughly what percentage of the earth's water is available for human consumption?

    a. About 97.5 per cent

    b. About 2.5 per cent

    c. About 1.75 per cent

    d. Less than 1 per cent

2 A common amoeba like *Amoeba proteus* reproduces by _____.

    a. Parthenogenesis   **b.** Binary Fission

    c. Pollination   **d.** Laying Eggs

3 Which Indian town hosts the largest cattle fair in Asia, where endangered birds and animals are also illegally sold and purchased?

    a. Sonepur   **b.** Howrah

    c. Coimbatore   **d.** Kandla

4 Charles Darwin spent around forty years studying the habits of this 'unsung creature' and published a book on his findings that sold thousands of copies. Which animal was this?

    a. Crow   **b.** Bee

    c. Earthworm   **d.** Mouse

Attempts by the British to contact the ancient hunter-gatherer tribe of the Andamanese, in order to tame them, doomed the tribe. They died in large numbers from diseases like measles and pneumonia, which they contracted from the outsiders, and against which they'd had no resistance.

5 What is a dendrologist's area of specialization?
 a. Fur and Hair **b.** Water
 c. Nerve Cells **d.** Trees

6 Due to the earth's curvature, the amount of solar energy received varies according to the _____.
 a. Longitude
 b. Latitude
 c. Altitude
 d. Depth

7 Where can one find India's only confirmed active volcano?
 a. Gujarat
 b. Himachal Pradesh
 c. Tamil Nadu
 d. Andaman and Nicobar Islands

8 Which documentary presenting Al Gore's campaign, released in 2006, raised international awareness about climate change and global warming?

a. *An Inconvenient Truth*

b. *Cool It*

c. *Monsoon: India's God of Life*

d. *March of the Penguins*

9 Biodiversity can be measured in terms of _____.

a. Genetic Diversity

b. Species Diversity

c. Ecosystem Diversity

d. All of these

10 Which famous conservationist was a founder member of WWF?

a. Sir Julian Huxley

b. Sir David Attenborough

c. Dr Salim Ali

d. Charles Darwin

In her book, *Snakeman: The Story of a Naturalist* (1990), Zai Whitaker writes about Natesan—an Irula tribal and expert snake tracker, who was a close friend of the well-known herpetologist, Romulus Whitaker. He could answer all of Romulus's questions about snakes and other reptiles of the area, many of which even college-trained naturalists and academics could not. Natesan spoke very little English, and his favourite expression was 'Sure, man!' He soon became known by a nickname—Sureman!

11 Which of these organisms belongs to the genus *Chaos*?

a. Coral

b. Giant Grouper

c. Killer Bee

d. Giant Amoeba

12 Which of these animals performs sexual cannibalism at times—a practice in which the female eats the male after mating with him?

a. Praying Mantis

b. Pufferfish

c. Great White Shark

d. Komodo Dragon

13 Some animals use bright colours as a defence mechanism to warn predators. What is this adaptation called?

a. Hybridization

b. Aposematism

c. Neoteny

d. Parasitism

The theme for World Environment Day on 5 June 2015 was 'Seven Billion Dreams. One Planet. Consume with Care'.

14 Which of these trios consists of greenhouse gases?

a. Methane, Carbon Dioxide, Nitrous Oxide

b. Nitrogen, Oxygen, Methane

c. Ozone, Carbon Monoxide, Argon

d. Water Vapour, CFCs, Nitrogen

15 Which of these animals is blue-blooded because of the copper content in its blood?

   a. Cuttlefish   **b.** Octopus

   c. Horseshoe Crab   **d.** All of these

16 Which of these animals has five pairs of heart-like organs that pump blood throughout its body?

   a. Earthworm   **b.** Blue Whale

   c. Octopus   **d.** California Condor

17 Which of these animals sometimes appears to fly, but, in fact, can only glide from one tree to the next?

   a. Squirrel

   b. Lizard

   c. Snake

   d. All of these

WWF-India shifted its headquarters from Mumbai to New Delhi, where land at Lodhi Estate was purchased from the Indian Government at a concessional rate. The building was made with the help of a generous donation from the Godrej Trust and the Godrej group of companies. The WWF-India Secretariat was inaugurated in 1989 by the then-President of India, R. Venkataraman. The event was attended by the president of WWF-International, Prince Philip, Duke of Edinburgh.

18 Nature and her adaptations are a never-ending source of inspiration to man. Man's imitation of nature for innovations to fulfil human needs is known as _____.

a. Bionics
b. Biomimetics
c. Biocontrol
d. Biogenesis

19 Which famous leader once said, 'The earth has enough resources for our need, but not for our greed.'

a. Barack Obama
b. Indira Gandhi
c. Nelson Mandela
d. Mahatma Gandhi

20 Counting all national parks, wildlife sanctuaries, and conservation and community reserves, how many Protected Areas are there in India currently?

a. Around 103
b. Around 531
c. Around 700
d. Around 916

21 Which of these animals has a carnivorous diet?

a. Marmot
b. Centipede
c. Millipede
d. Honeybee

22 Which of these organisms is not a parasite but an epiphyte i.e., it grows on another organism—using it for support—and obtains its own nutrition without harming its host?

a. Leech
b. Orchid
c. Fungus
d. Tapeworm

The Vyala, a mythical animal with a lion-like head, is often depicted in Indian art and architecture. It can be seen sculpted in stone at the Konark Sun Temple, Orissa, leaping over an elephant.

23 Which of these major rivers flows only in India during its entire course?

a. Ganga   **b.** Indus

c. Narmada   **d.** Brahmaputra

24 Produced by certain animals, which precious item contains nacre?

a. Coral   **b.** Pearl

c. Amber   **d.** Ambergris

25 Which Protected Area in the Indian subcontinent is no longer on the IUCN's 'List of World Heritage Sites in Danger' because of successful conservation action?

a. Lal Suhanra National Park, Pakistan

b. Manas National Park, India

c. Chitwan National Park, Nepal

d. Yala National Park, Sri Lanka

26 Which scientist is known as the father of the modern taxonomical system?

a. Charles Darwin   **b.** Carl Linnaeus

c. Aristotle   **d.** Ernst Mayr

27 Hard water, which is usually basic or alkaline, has a pH level higher than _____.

   a. 8.5　　　　　　　　　**b.** 9.5

   c. 10.5　　　　　　　　**d.** 11.5

28 Which Indian state has its own Wildlife (Protection) Act?

   a. Andaman and Nicobar Islands

   b. Daman and Diu

   c. National Capital Region of Delhi

   d. Jammu and Kashmir

Commonly called Caterpillar Fungus, the *Ophiocordyceps sinensis* is highly prized in Traditional Chinese Medicine and is used as treatment for a range of problems from cancer and AIDS to respiratory, heart, kidney and liver disease. More expensive than gold, it is found in the high-altitude areas of the Himalayas and the Tibetan Plateau. Unfortunately, it's now becoming rare due to overharvesting.

29 What characteristic do the Praying Mantis, the Bengal Tiger, the Himalayan Pied Woodpecker and the King Cobra have in common? They are all _____.

   a. Solitary

   b. Bloodthirsty

   c. Aerial

   d. Venomous

30 Wind power, unlike fossil fuels, generates electricity without emitting any greenhouse gases. It's renewable and abundantly available. What is India's global rank in installed wind-power capacity?

a. First
b. Fifth
c. Fifteenth
d. Fiftieth

31 Which Article of the Indian Constitution says that it is the duty of every Indian citizen 'to protect and improve the natural environment including forests, lakes, rivers and wildlife and to have compassion for living creatures'?

a. Article 21
b. Article 48
c. Article 51A
d. Article 48A

32 The Wildlife Crime Control Bureau (WCCB) of the Ministry of Environment, Forests and Climate Change (MoEFCC) combats organized wildlife crime in India. The bureau has regional offices in Delhi, Mumbai, Chennai, Kolkata and _____.

a. Srinagar
b. Jabalpur
c. Shillong
d. Thiruvananthapuram

33 Which of these has the status of a Wetland of International Importance, and is a designated Ramsar Site?

a. Keoladeo Ghana National Park
b. Loktak Lake
c. Chilika Lake
d. All of these

34 Arid, with a precipitation level below 400 mm, which is the world's largest desert?

   a. Sahara   **b.** Gobi

   c. Antarctica   **d.** Atacama

35 What is the term popularized by the Millennium Ecosystem Assessment (MA) for the economic value in the benefits gained from biodiversity by humans?

   a. Biodiversity Services

   b. Ecosystem Resources

   c. Ecosystem Services

   d. Biodiversity Bank

The term 'ecosystem', was first used by Arthur Tansley, to represent a group of living organisms (such as plants and animals) and non-living things (such as air, water and soil), as well as their interaction in the habitat in which they live and grow.

36 Which of these animals is a detritivore?

   a. Bee   **b.** Caterpillar

   c. Krait   **d.** Millipede

37 Who wrote the book, *On the Origin of Species* (1859)—the very foundation of evolutionary biology?

   a. Carl Linnaeus

   b. Charles Darwin

   c. J.B.S. Haldane

   d. Gregor Mendel

38 In 2015, the 21st session of the Conference of the Parties (COP21) of the UN Framework Convention on Climate Change (UNFCCC) took place in _____.

   a. New Delhi   **b.** Rio de Janeiro

   c. Vladivostok   **d.** Paris

39 Which of these prey animals produces ultrasonic clicks that can jam a bat's echolocation system?

   a. Bush Frog   **b.** Tiger Moth

   c. Dormouse   **d.** House Gecko

In a survey carried out in November 2015 in the United Kingdom, Charles Darwin's *On the Origin of Species* (1859) was selected as the most important educational book ever written!

40 Which is India's largest freshwater lake and also a Ramsar Site?

   a. Wular Lake   **b.** Chilika Lake

   c. Pangong Tso   **d.** Vembanad Kol

41 What is the term used to describe the capture and storage of excess carbon dioxide that is released by human activities? This is done to mitigate global warming.

   a. Carbon Footprint   **b.** Carbon Credit

   c. Carbon Depletion   **d.** Carbon Sequestration

42 Which Indian state has the largest installed capacity for solar power?

    a. West Bengal   **b.** Rajasthan

    c. Madhya Pradesh   **d.** Andhra Pradesh

43 Which eminent Supreme Court lawyer and Magsaysay Award-winner has won several landmark victories for preserving the environment, such as the Taj Mahal case, the Ganges pollution case, and the environmental education and awareness case, among others?

    a. Shekhar Singh   **b.** Medha Patkar

    c. M.C. Mehta   **d.** Ritwick Dutta

44 Just like your surname and first name, scientific names—also called Latin names—of living things have two parts. What do they denote?

    a. Family and Genus   **b.** Genus and Species

    c. Order and Family   **d.** Class and Order

45 Protecting this species protects the habitat and all species that inhabit it. What is such a species known as?

    a. Flagship Species

    b. Umbrella Species

    c. Indicator Species

    d. Invasive Species

46 Three of these animals are endemic to the Indian subcontinent and listed as Critically Endangered by the IUCN. Since it is also found in a few other parts of Asia besides India, which one is listed as Vulnerable?

a. Malabar Civet
b. Great Indian Bustard
c. Indian Vulture
d. Red Panda

47 Which of these acts as the world's largest carbon sink, wherein chemicals containing carbon are absorbed and stored?

a. Forests
b. Soil
c. Oceans
d. Wetlands

48 Which of these is the classic reference book by S.H. Prater, originally published in 1939?

a. *Birds of the Indian Subcontinent*
b. *The Book of Indian Trees*
c. *The Book of Indian Animals*
d. *The Book of Indian Reptiles and Amphibians* .

49 What is the name of the Bombay Natural History Society's office in Mumbai?

a. Salim Ali House
b. Tiger Trust
c. Wildlife Institute
d. Hornbill House

Did you know that Lavkumar Khachar (1931–2015)
was a famous naturalist and one of the pioneers

of WWF-India's nature-education and awareness activities?

50 Which is the lowest pass in the Western Ghats? It influences south India's climate by allowing the moisture-laden southwest monsoons and cyclonic winds from the Bay of Bengal to pass through.

  a. Palghat Gap   **b.** Haldighati Pass

  c. Amba Ghat   **d.** Bhor Ghat

51 Which Indian ruler of the 3rd Century BC formulated some of the earliest wildlife protection laws in the world?

  a. King Dasharatha   **b.** King Pandu

  c. Emperor Ashok   **d.** Emperor Akbar

52 Which of these gliding animals can be seen in India?

  a. Flying Frogs

  b. Flying Lizards

  c. Flying Snakes

  d. All of these

53 What is the study of earthquakes known as?

  a. Seismology   **b.** Paleontology

  c. Meteorology   **d.** Trichology

54 A caecilian is a type of _____.

  a. Reptile   **b.** Insect

  c. Amphibian   **d.** Fish

55 A number of birds and mammals exhibit anti-predatory behaviour that involves coordinated watchfulness, known as _____.

a. Maternal Behaviour   **b.** Herd Behaviour

c. Sentinel Behaviour   **d.** Flight or Fight Behaviour

56 Which of these animals is a hermaphrodite i.e., it has both male and female reproductive organs?

a. Snail

b. Earthworm

c. Nudibranch

d. All of these

57 What is the outermost atmospheric layer called?

a. Exosphere   **b.** Lithosphere

c. Troposphere   **d.** Thermosphere

58 So far, how many wetland sites in India have been designated as Wetlands of International Importance by the Ramsar Convention?

a. Fifteen   **b.** Twenty-six

c. Thirty-seven   **d.** Forty-eight

59 Soft water, which is usually corrosive, has a pH level less than _____.

a. 6.5   **b.** 7.5

c. 8.5   **d.** 9.5

60 Which of these renewable energy sources is not solar in origin?

   a. Wind

   b. Biomass

   c. Deep Geothermal

   d. Water

Have you ever heard the spine-chilling cry of the Forest Eagle-owl, which sometimes sounds like a human in distress? C.F. Gordon Cumming described it as,

'A shriek of torture, followed by a gurgling sound as if a victim were being strangled; then follow piercing screams and convulsive cries agonizing to hear, so suggestive are they of murder; then follows a silence as of death, perhaps broken once more by dismal wails and pitiful cries. It is a voice so very eerie that it is said no one can hear it without a shudder, and all natives hold it in superstitious horror, believing it to be a warning of death.'

61 Who is the current Minister of Environment, Forests and Climate Change in the Government of India?

   a. Jairam Ramesh

   b. Jayanthi Natarajan

   c. Maneka Gandhi

   d. Prakash Javadekar

62 Through how many Indian states does the River Ganga flow?
- **a.** Three
- **b.** Five
- **c.** Nine
- **d.** Eleven

63 Involved in venom extraction in order to produce the antidote for snakebite victims, which ethnic group of south India is also known to be expert snake-catchers?
- **a.** Jarawa
- **b.** Pardhi
- **c.** Bawariya
- **d.** Irula

64 Which male marine animal leaves land at birth and doesn't return for the rest of its life?
- **a.** Dugong
- **b.** Crab
- **c.** Sea Turtle
- **d.** Sea Snake

65 In recent years, where in Asia have a sneezing monkey, a walking fish, a jewel-like snake and 200 other biological treasures been discovered?
- **a.** Eastern Himalayas
- **b.** Thar Desert
- **c.** Pamir Mountains
- **d.** Kamchatka Peninsula

66 Which chemical—a harmful air pollutant at ground level—acts as a shield for the environment, as well as for humans, against the damaging ultraviolet radiation of the sun?
- **a.** Ozone
- **b.** Chlorine
- **c.** Carbon Dioxide
- **d.** Chlorofluorocarbon

67 What is the distance between the earth and the sun?

    a. About 173 million km   **b.** About 150 million km

    c. About 100 million km   **d.** About 93 million km

> In geological terms, the Himalayas, a natural barrier to the north of India, are *young* mountains—they are *only* about fifty million years old! They are the birthplace of important Asian rivers, including the Indus, the Ganga and the Brahmaputra, that provide water to around forty crore Indians. We need to respect and preserve the Himalayan ecosystem.

68 Which is the largest riverine island in India?

    a. Majuli   **b.** Sundarban

    c. Mumbai   **d.** Diu

69 India has a network of Protected Areas; of these, how many have been given the status of a national park?

    a. 66   **b.** 103

    c. 275   **d.** 531

70 Which environmental scientist coined the term 'biodiversity hotspot' as a conservation prioritizing tool?

    a. Norman Myers   **b.** Rachael Carson

    c. John Muir   **d.** Jane Goodall

71 Which Article of the Indian Constitution gives the directive that 'the State shall endeavour to protect and improve the environment and to safeguard the forests and wildlife of the country'?
a. Article 42
b. Article 48
c. Article 51A
d. Article 48A

72 Which programme launched by the United Nations in 2007 aims to tackle climate change and to help slow down biodiversity loss by reducing emissions from deforestation and the degradation of forests?
a. REDD
b. CCP
c. COP
d. Kyoto Protocol

73 On which of the following sub-islands of the Andaman and Nicobar Islands is an active volcano located?
a. North Andaman Island
b. Barren Island
c. Car Nicobar
d. Ross Island

Kailash Sankhala, the noted tiger conservationist and former head of Project Tiger in 1973, wrote,

'Animals know that unlike man, the tiger is satisfied with what he has killed for the day and is not concerned with tomorrow. He takes only what he needs and does not kill for the sake of killing. There is a perfect understanding between predator and prey. For the first time I felt ashamed of being a man, who is not even trusted by the jackals, much less the deer and antelopes.'

Isn't it terrible that humans usually kill for sport or out of greed for more?

74 Biogas, a renewable energy source, is primarily a combination of methane and which other gas?

a. Oxygen   **b.** Carbon Dioxide

c. Sulphide   **d.** None of these

75 Which of these lakes—located in north Sikkim and one of the highest wetlands in the state—is sacred to Buddhists, Hindus and Sikhs?

a. Tsomgo lake   **b.** Pangong Tso

c. Lakshmi Pokhari Lake   **d.** Gurudongmar Lake

76 The vent in the earth's crust that periodically ejects a column of hot water and steam is known as _____.

a. Hot Spring

b. Fissure

c. Geyser

d. Fumarole

77 Which of these is an endangered aboriginal forest tribe of the Andaman and Nicobar Islands, that has, till now, shunned all contact with the outside world?

a. Great Andamanese   **b.** Jarawa

c. Onge   **d.** Sentinelese

WWF's Living Planet Report in 2014 estimated that natural resources produced by 1.5 earths would be needed to meet with people's demands each year. Unless we use less and make better choices about how we live our lives, our planet—and all living things that inhabit it—will face a grave future.

78 Acid rain can have harmful effects on plants, animals and the infrastructure. Which of these acids is the main cause of its corrosive properties?

a. Carbonic Acid

b. Boric Acid

c. Hydrochloric Acid

d. Sulphuric Acid

79 The depletion of the ozone layer over the earth's polar regions has created the _____.

a. Greenhouse Effect

b. Ozone Hole

c. El Niño

d. All of these

80 In which year was the international, non-governmental conservation organization, World Wildlife Fund, formed, at the then headquarters of the IUCN, in Morges, Switzerland?

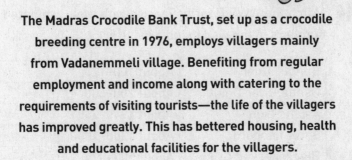

a. 1941
b. 1951
c. 1961
d. 1971

The Madras Crocodile Bank Trust, set up as a crocodile breeding centre in 1976, employs villagers mainly from Vadanemmeli village. Benefiting from regular employment and income along with catering to the requirements of visiting tourists—the life of the villagers has improved greatly. This has bettered housing, health and educational facilities for the villagers.

81 Globally, what is the most widely observed impact of climate change?

a. Cyclones
b. Increased rise in sea level
c. Acid Rain
d. None of the above

82 Who wrote *The Man-eating Leopard of Rudraprayag* (1947)?

a. Kenneth Anderson
b. Jim Corbett
c. Valmik Thapar
d. Billy Arjan Singh

83 Match these endemic wild animals with their respective countries:

Platypus	New Zealand
Lion-tailed Macaque	Madagascar
Marine Iguana	Australia
Kakapo	Galapagos Islands
Aye-aye	India

84 Match the WWF Priority Species with their estimated numbers in the wild in India in 2015:

Bengal Tiger	About 100–125
Ganga River Dolphin	About 200–600
Asiatic Lion	About 1945–2491
Snow Leopard	About 1200–1800
Black-necked Crane	About 500–525

**One of the first readers of Dr Salim Ali's book,
The Book of Indian Birds (1941), was Pandit
Jawaharlal Nehru, who got a signed copy for his
daughter, Indira.**

85 Match the animal with its main food:

Flying Fox	Ants
Pangolin	Snakes
Green Sea Turtle	Sponges
Hawksbill Turtle	Seagrass
King Cobra	Fruit

86 Match the Indian wildlife species with the state where it is found:

Red Deer	Andhra Pradesh
Red Line Torpedo Barb	Jammu and Kashmir
Red Sanders	Kerala
Red Panda	Manipur
Red Vanda	Sikkim

87 Match these wild animals with their sanctuary homes:

Irrawaddy Dolphin	Great Himalayan National Park
Giant Grizzled Squirrel	Manas National Park
Indian Skimmer	Nalaban Wildlife Sanctuary
Western Tragopan	Bhimshankar Wildlife Sanctuary
Pygmy Hog	National Chambal Sanctuary

Have you heard of Suleman Patel? He was a photographer who became famous for his amazing shot which showed eleven lions in a single frame, drinking water at the Gir National Park. You should take a look at it too!

88 Match the conservationists with their conservation work /movement:

Dr Vandana Shiva	Narmada Bachao Andolan
Gaura Devi	Navdanya: Seed Sovereignty
Medha Patkar	Chipko Movement
Jane Goodall	WWF-India, Founder Trustee
Anne Wright	Roots & Shoots

89 Brightly coloured and graceful, what kind of an animal is a nudibranch?

90 After which ancient tribe of the Andaman and Nicobar Islands has a Protected Area been named?

91 Fossils of the *Rajasaurus*, a large carnivorous dinosaur with a strange head-crest, were found in India between 1982 and 1984. In which river valley were they found?

92 Against which dam did Medha Patkar start the Narmada Bachao Andolan protest? Reports estimate that the dam, upon completion, would submerge about 37,000 hectares of forest, tribal and agricultural land.

93 Which government body was established on 1 July 1916 to promote the survey, exploration and research of the fauna in India? Its parent body, the MoEFCC, was created much later, in 1985.

94 Which famous conservationist, who lived at Gurney House, famously wrote in 1944,
'The tiger is a large-hearted gentleman with boundless courage and that when he is exterminated, as exterminated he will be, unless public opinion rallies to his support—India will be the poorer by having lost the finest of her fauna'?

The tiger is worshipped in many cultures, including that of the Warlis, an ancient tribe in western India, who are now world-famous for their art. They call the tiger god Vaghya or Vaghadeva.

95 After the Bhopal gas tragedy in 1984, which landmark law was enacted by the Indian Government in 1986?

96 Whose popular book about the animals of Seeonee Hills—wolves, bears, jackals and more—conveyed moral lessons and was used by Lord Baden-Powell's Cub Scouts as a motivational book?

97 What kind of animals are the Common Leopard, Blue Pansy, Striped Tiger, Painted Lady, Common Gull and Common Jay?

98 What kind of animal is the Spanish Dancer?

In the 1960s, the agenda of conservation organizations was saving species—with a special focus on large animals like the elephant, tiger and rhino. Today, we understand that conservation is about so much more—entire habitats and ecosystems have to be protected! Furthermore, for the success of any conservation project, people and their needs—especially those living close to Protected Areas—have to be included as well. Don't you think so too?

99 Who wrote *Tigers For Dinner: Tall Tales by Jim Corbett's Khansama* (2013), a book full of amusing stories about cobras, crocodiles, man-eating tigers, useless maharajas, haunting pillows and lost kitchen boys?

100 'To develop and maintain an international network of wetlands which are important for the conservation of

global biological diversity and for sustaining human life through the ecological and hydrological functions they perform'
—this is the guiding vision of the Ramsar Convention. In which country is the city of Ramsar?

101 Where in India is 'Jhum', a primitive method of cultivation, still practised?

The word 'sonar' is actually derived from the phrase 'Sound Navigation And Ranging'. It's the use of sound waves for direction-finding, locating objects as well as communication. This technology is now used by people in submarines and deep-sea fishing vessels, but has been used for hundreds of years by animals like dolphins and bats.

102 A species of flora or fauna that is found only in one particular ecosystem, and nowhere else, is known as _____.

103 The Living Planet Index is an accepted method of assessing the earth's biodiversity and documenting its rapid decline. According to the LPI of 2014, what is the percentage of decline among vertebrate species between the years 1970–2010?

Do you know that all life on our planet—including all plants, animals, water, soil and air—exists as a connected community in a thin layer around the earth? It's called the biosphere. Nothing and no one exists independently.

104 To which country did Carl Linnaeus, who formulated the modern taxonomical naming system, belong?

105 The Giant Panda is the recognized symbol for the wildlife conservation movement. Which species is the symbol for extinction?

Answers

1. d. **Less than 1 per cent**

2. b. **Binary Fission**
    Binary fission is a form of asexual reproduction. The original cell multiplies, by dividing itself to produce two copies. These will further subdivide to produce more and more cells. Bacteria usually multiply in this way.

3. a. **Sonepur**
    Held in Bihar, the Sonepur Cattle Fair takes place according to the Hindu calendar, during the full moon period every November and lasts for a fortnight or longer. Although culturally important, this fair is also a hub for illegal wildlife trade. A number of wildlife conservation NGOs, such as TRAFFIC India, have conducted surveys and raids at the fair, documenting the trade of several animals, including that of species protected under the

Wildlife (Protection) Act. These include thousands of animals, from species of birds like falcons, Shikhras, parakeets, mynas, munias, and exotic birds, to mammals like elephants, Nilgais, langurs, macaques, porcupines, mongoose and more. Due to the awful conditions in which the animals are kept captive, many of them die even before they are sold; their bodies are carelessly thrown aside, which creates a horrible stench. It's necessary for authorities to take firm action and punish such traders who break the law.

4. **c. Earthworm**

Charles Darwin was fascinated by earthworms and their behaviour, and studied how this insignificant creature was able to create rich and productive soil through its digestive processes. He published numerous papers about earthworms and, after studying them for around forty years, he published his bestselling book, *The Formation of Vegetable Mould Through the Action of Worms, with Observations on Their Habits* (1881). He kept earthworms in pots, and wrote in detail about his experiments to gauge their reaction to noise and light. He also maintained records of the way in which the worms pulled leaves into their burrows.

5. **d. Trees**

6. **b. Latitude**

7. **d. Andaman and Nicobar Islands**

8. **a.** *An Inconvenient Truth*

This is an award-winning film that played a key role in raising public awareness about the dangerous reality of human-induced—anthropogenic—climate change. Directed by Davis Guggenheim, the film records Al Gore's campaign to inform the masses about global warming and the greenhouse effect. Some incidents in Al Gore's life, such as his interactions with climate expert Roger Revelle, the death of his sister due to lung cancer, and the near-death of his son, prompted him to start this campaign. Gore is founder of The Alliance for Climate Protection and won the Nobel Peace Prize in 2007.

9. **d. All of these**

10. **a. Sir Julian Huxley**

11. **d. Giant Amoeba**

12. **a. Praying Mantis**

Many species of arachnids and insects have developed a practice in which the female eats her partner before, during or after mating. There are several explanations for this kind of behaviour. Experts suggest that in some species this could be a way by which the female improves her physical condition and her chances of reproducing, and also compensates for the lack of other available prey. It could also be a demonstration of the female's aggression after mating. Some studies show that the males of some species make the ultimate sacrifice of being eaten by the female to ensure the quality and number of their unborn offspring.

13. **b. Aposematism**

Several animals—and some plants too—use eye-catching colours and patterns to signal that they are dangerous to others. Plant berries, bugs, butterflies, frogs, snakes and others use the colour crimson or red in bold patterns, spots, splotches and stripes to indicate that they are poisonous and should be left alone. Other species, which are actually not poisonous, sometimes mimic the dangerous ones to fool their predators.

14. **a. Methane, Carbon Dioxide, Nitrous Oxide**

15. **d. All of these**

16. **a. Earthworm**

17. **d. All of these**

Volant animals are those that are built for aerial locomotion and can either fly or glide. Birds, bats and insects have powered flight, while several other animals merely glide. Most land animals that glide are arboreal, and live mainly in tree canopies. They glide from one tree to the next, mainly to escape from predators and to forage for food. Besides squirrels, snakes and lizards, there are many others who have adopted this unique way of moving around.

18. b. Biomimetics

The human study of copying or mimicking nature's materials, designs and structures to develop products that improve modern life is called biomimetics. This includes huge inventions like airplanes and helicopters as well as smaller ones like Velcro, and swimwear that mimics the hydrodynamic structure of sharkskin.

19. d. Mahatma Gandhi

20. c. Around 700

21. b. Centipede

22. b. Orchid

23. c. Narmada

24. b. Pearl

Nacre, also called Mother of Pearl, is an iridescent, hard, mineral-like substance that is secreted by some molluscs inside their shell. Layers of nacre secreted by the oyster over time forms a pearl. Tiny particles, like a grain of sand, sometimes get lodged in the oyster shell. This causes irritation to the soft body of the oyster, which then covers it over and over again with layers of smooth, shiny nacre. This happens naturally too, but nowadays, most pearls are cultured—humans insert some form of irritant into the oyster to induce it to produce nacre to form a pearl. Natural pearls are usually more expensive than cultured ones.

25. b. Manas National Park, India

Manas National Park has several unique species including the Assam Roofed Turtle, the Golden Langur, the Hispid Hare, the Pygmy Hog, the Indian Rhinoceros, the Asian Elephant and the Bengal Tiger, among others. Earlier, in 1992, the sanctuary was included in the List of World Heritage Sites in Danger. But in 2011, it was delisted since the wildlife was considered to be recovering well post the damages incurred during a period of ethnic unrest.

26. b. Carl Linnaeus

Scientists have organized all living organisms into groups according to certain physical characteristics that they share. The large groups are further subdivided into smaller groups with more closely shared characteristics. The scientific study of this kind of classification is called taxonomy. The broad classifications that are most widely accepted for plants and animals are kingdom, phylum, class, order, family, genus and species. The person who was the first to use such a system and lay down its rules was Carl Linnaeus. Today, science follows Linnaeus's system of giving biological names to plants and animals.

27. a. 8.5

28. d. Jammu and Kashmir

29. a. Solitary

Different animals have developed different, characteristic behaviour patterns according to their habitat and needs. Some animals have evolved to live in groups, while others best survive alone for most of their lives. Adult animals that live alone, except for mating and raising their young, are called solitary. Many solitary animals aggressively compete with their own species for food, territory and mates.

30. b. Fifth

31. c. Article 51A

32. b. Jabalpur
The WCCB is a government body designated to gather information about, and work with government enforcement agencies to prevent, investigate and punish crimes against wild plants and animals. It has to remain aware and alert at all times, maintaining a network of informers who can tip officials off about wildlife crimes, like the illegal killing of an elephant or the chopping down of a Red Sanders tree, preferably before they happen. It has to be up-to-date with the latest trends in demand as well as the modus operandi in illegal international trade networks; it also has to help train forest officials as well as police and customs personnel. Additionally, the body helps frame policies to curb wildlife crimes.

33. d. All of these

34. c. Antarctica

35. c. Ecosystem Services
Although humans have realized since ancient times that all their primary needs can be fulfilled by nature,

254

they have still done a poor job of protecting it. Money and power have surpassed nature in importance. The concept of ecosystem services has been developed by conservationists and scientists so that people understand the benefits from nature in monetary terms and can also better assess the loss incurred through damage to biodiversity. The broad visible services or benefits that we receive from nature are as follows:

- Supporting services, which include nutrient recycling and soil formation benefits.
- Provisioning services, which include food, clothing, shelter and energy benefits.
- Regulating services, which include climate regulation, clean water and air benefits.
- Cultural services, which include cultural, spiritual, recreational, scientific and educational benefits.

The audit of the monetary value of each of these benefits is known as The Economics of Ecosystems and Biodiversity (TEEB).

36. d. Millipede

37. b. Charles Darwin

38. d. Paris

39. b. Tiger Moth

40. a. Wular Lake

41. d. **Carbon Sequestration**

42. b. **Rajasthan**

43. c. **M.C. Mehta**

   Mr. M.C. Mehta is a well-known environmentalist. In the environmental education and awareness case—that Mehta won—the court ordered cinema halls to exhibit two slides about the environment at every show, and television channels to broadcast a five-to-seven-minute-long environment programme besides a weekly one. Since the year 1992, education about the environment has become a compulsory subject in schools, with the University Grants Commission (UGC) introducing it as a course at the university-level as well.

44. b. **Genus and Species**

45. b. **Umbrella Species**

   Conservationists have coined this term for a protected animal—usually one that is big and well-recognized—which normally needs a large habitat and other accompanying species within the same habitat for its survival. Protecting the one large species naturally provides an umbrella of protection to several other species and the habitat. The tiger is an example of umbrella species.

46. d. **Red Panda**

47. c. **Oceans**

48. c. *The Book of Indian Animals*

49. d. Hornbill House

50. a. Palghat Gap

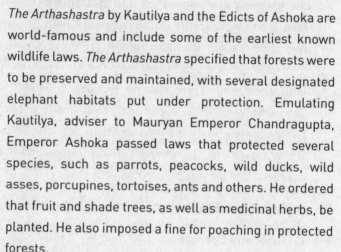

51. c. Emperor Ashok

The Arthashastra by Kautilya and the Edicts of Ashoka are world-famous and include some of the earliest known wildlife laws. *The Arthashastra* specified that forests were to be preserved and maintained, with several designated elephant habitats put under protection. Emulating Kautilya, adviser to Mauryan Emperor Chandragupta, Emperor Ashoka passed laws that protected several species, such as parrots, peacocks, wild ducks, wild asses, porcupines, tortoises, ants and others. He ordered that fruit and shade trees, as well as medicinal herbs, be planted. He also imposed a fine for poaching in protected forests.

52. d. All of these

53. a. Seismology

54. c. Amphibian

55. c. Sentinel Behaviour

56. d. All of these

57. a. Exosphere

58. b. Twenty-six

The Ramsar Convention, which came into force in 1975, is an international treaty signed by various countries for the preservation and sustainable use of important wetland habitats. So far, 169 countries from across the globe—including India—have signed this treaty. In many countries, unfortunately, wetlands are treated as wastelands, and are drained for developmental activities.

59. a. 6.5

60. c. Deep Geothermal

61. d. Prakash Javadekar

62. b. Five

63. d. Irula

The Irulas, an ancient tribe of south India, traditionally performed the important task of pest control in early Dravidian kingdoms. They live in Tamil Nadu and Kerala, and are skilled snake- and rat-catchers. Before the Wildlife (Protection) Act was constituted, Irulas earned a living by supplying snakeskins for the export market. However, after its implementation, they lost their means of livelihood and, although they are experts in their field of knowledge with excellent snake-tracking abilities, they were forced to work as unskilled labourers. With the start of the Irula Snake-Catchers Industrial Cooperative Society (ISCICS) and the Irula Tribe Women's Welfare

Society (ITWWS), they now have a more sustainable means of income.

64. c. Sea Turtle

65. a. Eastern Himalayas
From 2009 to 2014, around 211 new species have been discovered by scientists in the Eastern Himalayas—one of the richest biodiversity areas on earth. In the last six years, a new primate, a new bird species, a snake, ten amphibian species, around twenty-six fish and about 133 species of plants were found in this region. Earlier, between 1998 and 2008, around 354 new species were discovered here. Sadly, however, the region is being degraded and destroyed rapidly, with some estimates claiming that only 25 per cent of the habitats remain. It seems certain that many species will be lost even before they are discovered.

66. a. Ozone

67. b. About 150 million km

68. a. Majuli

69. b. 103

70. a. Norman Myers

71. d. Article 48A

72. a. REDD or Reducing Emissions from Deforestation and Forest Degradation

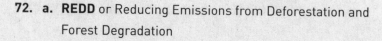

POTPOURRIxPOTPOURRI

259

73. b. Barren Island

The uninhabited, volcanic Barren Island, part of the Andaman and Nicobar chain, erupts periodically—with its first documented eruption dating back to 1787. Based on satellite images, the Darwin Volcanic Ash Advisory Centre (VAAC) has reported that recently, in February 2016, the volcano spewed ash plumes about one and a half kilometres in height, from its caldera.

74. b. Carbon Dioxide

75. d. Gurudongmar Lake

76. c. Geyser

77. d. Sentinelese

A part of India, the North Sentinel Island is a tiny coral island in the Bay of Bengal, to the west of the South Andaman Islands. The island is home to the Sentinelese people, an endangered native tribe of Negroid descent. They are completely isolated from the outside world and treat any attempt to contact them with hostility, using primitive weapons like bows, arrows and javelins against visitors and helicopters. This isolation is one of the reasons that they have managed to survive and preserve their ancient culture. They are not immune to our diseases and, when a few members of the tribe were kidnapped in the 19th century and taken to Port Blair, some got sick very quickly and died. There could be as few as around fifty to 500 Sentinelese left, but there is no way of getting a correct estimate. After the terrible tsunami in 2004, it was thought that the tribe may have been wiped out, but they were later spotted by the Indian Navy's rescue helicopters. It is possible that the tribe used ancient indigenous knowledge that helped them survive.

78. d. Sulphuric Acid

79. b. Ozone Hole

80. c. 1961

81. b. Increased rise in sea level

82. b. Jim Corbett

While most of his writings on man-eaters were about tigers, his famous story about the man-eater of Rudraprayag told of a large, old male leopard. When Corbett finally killed the leopard in 1926, he found that it had a grey muzzle, no whiskers, worn-out teeth and a broken canine. He deduced that, due to old age, the leopard had probably started scavenging on dead bodies and had developed a taste for human flesh due to scarcity of its natural prey. This was possible because of easy access to human flesh due to the 1918 cholera epidemic as well as cremations on the banks of the Ganga. Furthermore, Rudraprayag, in the Garhwal Himalayas, is on an ancient pilgrimage route and attracts many devotees. This leopard is said to have killed around 125 people in eight years, between 1918 and 1926. A plaque in present-day Rudraprayag marks the place where it was killed.

83.

Platypus	Australia
Lion-tailed Macaque	India
Marine Iguana	Galapagos Islands
Kakapo	New Zealand
Aye-aye	Madagascar

84.

Bengal Tiger	About 1945–2491
Ganga River Dolphin	About 1200–1800
Asiatic Lion	About 500–525
Snow Leopard	About 200–600
Black-necked Crane	About 100–125

85.

Flying Fox	Fruit
Pangolin	Ants
Green Sea Turtle	Seagrass
Hawksbill Turtle	Sponges
King Cobra	Snakes

86.

Red Deer	Jammu and Kashmir
Red Line Torpedo Barb	Kerala
Red Sanders	Andhra Pradesh
Red Panda	Sikkim
Red Vanda	Manipur

87.

Irrawaddy Dolphin	Nalaban Wildlife Sanctuary
Giant Grizzled Squirrel	Bhimshankar Wildlife Sanctuary
Indian Skimmer	National Chambal Sanctuary
Western Tragopan	Great Himalayan National Park
Pygmy Hog	Manas National Park

88.

Vandana Shiva	Navdanya: Seed Sovereignty
Gaura Devi	Chipko Movement
Medha Patkar	Narmada Bachao Andolan
Jane Goodall	Roots & Shoots
Anne Wright	WWF-India, Founder Trustee

89. Sea Slug

90. Jarawas

91. Narmada Valley

The rocks of the Narmada basin, in Madhya Pradesh and Gujarat, are rich in fossils. Well-preserved fossilized bones of the *Rajasaurus narmadensis*, set in limestone rock-sediments in this area, were a major find. Round limestone formations were found in Rahioli, Gujarat, during a survey by the Geological Survey of India (GSI); these turned out to be dinosaur eggs. Parts of the skeleton were also found in Gujarat and in Jabalpur, Madhya Pradesh. This new dinosaur species, found only in India, is said to be related to a dinosaur from Madagascar; it was announced as a joint study conducted by scientists from GSI, the University of Chicago and others. Today, you can see the enormous reconstructed skull of the Rajasaurus in the Indian Museum in Kolkata.

92. Sardar Sarovar Dam

93. Zoological Survey of India

94. Jim Corbett

95. The Environment (Protection) Act, 1986

96. Rudyard Kipling's *The Jungle Book* (1894)

97. Butterflies

98. Nudibranch

99. Ruskin Bond

100. Iran

101. Northeast India

Jhum is a primitive form of shifting agriculture, practised in the Neolithic Age by nomadic hunter-gatherer clans. Forests or grasslands were chopped and burned, in order to clear space to grow crops of edible plants. After the soil nutrients were exhausted at one location, the tribe moved to another part of the forest and repeated the process. Although the 'slash and burn' technique results in deforestation, soil erosion, biodiversity loss and production of greenhouse gases, it is still practised in parts of the tropics, particularly in tribal areas. In Indonesia, large forest areas are cleared in this manner, for the purpose of palm oil cultivation. In India, Jhum cultivation is practised mainly in the forested hill slopes of Northeast India.

102. Endemic Species

An endemic animal or plant, found only in a particular region, may be restricted to a large or small area—a country or even just a tiny pocket. For example, the Lion-tailed Macaque is a primate species endemic to the Western Ghats in south India whereas lemurs are a group of primates endemic to the island of Madagascar.

103. 52 per cent

The Living Planet Report, published by WWF and available as an online resource, includes the LPI, which is a scientific analysis that shows the decrease of land, freshwater and marine vertebrate species. The latest

LPI, published in 2014, shows that in forty years (1970–2010), freshwater vertebrate species have dwindled by 76 per cent, and both land-dwelling as well as marine vertebrate species have dwindled by 39 per cent. Overall, the percentage of decline is 52 per cent. It also indicates that the rate of decline of biodiversity is highest in the tropics.

104. Sweden

105. Dodo

The Dodo is a bird from the pigeon family and its closest living relative is said to be the Nicobar Pigeon. All that is known about the Dodo is mainly from pictures and a collection of bones—that it was a large, flightless bird that lived on the island of Mauritius, and that it was doomed with the arrival of Portuguese and Dutch sailors in the early 17th century, who brought along rats, pigs, dogs and cats with them. Hungry for fresh meat, the sailors and their animals hunted the Dodo with ease. It could not fly and had no natural defences against humans as it lived on an island that had previously been free from predators. Because of its unique appearance, some live birds were even sent to Europe and Asia. The popular book *Alice's Adventures in Wonderland* (1865), by Lewis Carroll, features a Dodo as one of the characters.

Wild in the Backyard
Arefa Tehsin

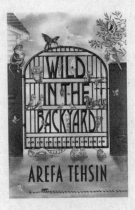

Enter the secret world of your wild neighbours!

Ever wondered why this world's called a rat race? Why does your teacher call you the chatter bird of the class? Who is the venomous hundred legger who lives in your bathroom?

Let's find out the answers to these and other questions in this exciting, one-of-a-kind backyard-jungle book. Wilderness and wildlife aren't just confined to the forests; there is a whole lot of wild in our own backyards! Some of these critters are awake with us in the day. Others wake up when we go to bed . . .

Discover the hunters and the hunted, the diggers and the tunnellers, the raptors and the roaches roaming around under our very noses.

Say hi to them and take a look at their home, which, incidentally, is also ours.

Become a Junior Inventor
Nikhil Gumbhir

Imagine, Invent, Engineer!

Ever wondered how roller coasters work? Been fascinated with nuts, bolts, screwdrivers, batteries, switches, wires and bulbs? Get acquainted with these movers and shakers of the world of gadgetry around us . . . and become a Junior Inventor yourself!

Put together by Cloud Mentor, a company that guides kids to become budding inventors, this fun book is specially designed for today's readers and has tons of activities to keep them happily occupied. Featuring almost every conceivable topic of interest—from machines, circuits, kitchen innovations to design basics—this incredible book helps children unleash their creativity and innovative best.

Learn how to make an automobile run, create your own traffic light at home and explore the science behind your favourite remote-controlled toy. Work on these supercool DIY experiments and more, discover some amazing facts and experience the magic of science like never before!